DRAW

SPACES

John Chambers

Homer's The Odyssey

ISBN 979-12-201-4026-3
First edition: May 2023

Edited by Stella Fusca

Homer's The Odyssey

Dedication

To Mary, Sarah, and Thérèse,

with all my love.

νόστος

Acknowledgment

Karen Fox, Pat Deeley, Ger Sullivan, Ed Jarvis and Anne Chambers

Ginevra Picani, Elisa Giuliani, Stella Fusca, Antonio Maggini and the Europe Books team.

The Odyssey is a strange adventure tale of a grown man trying to get home after fighting in a war.

He's on that long journey home, and it's filled with traps and pitfalls.

He's cursed to wander...In a lot of ways, some of these same things have happened to you.

You too have had drugs dropped into your wine.

You too have shared a bed with the wrong woman.

You too have been spellbound by magical voices, sweet voices with strange melodies.

You too have come so far and have been so far blown back.

And you've had close calls as well.

You have angered people you should not have.

And you too have rambled this country all around.

And you've also felt that ill wind, the one that blows you no good.

Bob Dylan
Nobel Lecture 2017

Introduction

This amazing sonnet sequence by John Chambers is a masterful retelling of one man's extraordinary journey to his home. Homer's Odyssey stands as a cornerstone of western culture. In 2018, when the BBC conducted a survey of experts around the world to find literature's most important and enduring narrative, the Odyssey topped the list.

Chambers' translation of this classic in the form of a sonnet sequence is an astonishing achievement. The verse is vibrant and vivid, written in a style that is totally accessible to the modern ready and yet faithful to the original text. The story is charged through with poetic energy, clarity and precision.

As they sailed, their passenger, unaware
slept deep and dreamless. He, who for twenty years
faced trials in skirmishes and brute warfare
on land and sea - a hero among peers
slept serenely on board the bucking ship.
Like a four horse team who wait impatiently
to surge ahead at the first touch of the whip
so ran that craft, riding across the sea.
Right through the night she arrowed on her way,
faster than a falcon in downwind flight
[the fastest of all sea birds so they say]
and reached Ithaca in dawn's rose coloured light.
They chose a sheltered cave in which to land
and with careful skill eased her up on sand.

Its gripping story and timeless characters are so vivid that this 3,000-year-old tale has never been eclipsed. Its very title has become embedded in our culture to describe an epic, difficult journey.

It is rare to find a translation of this great classic that seems so effortless and yet so learned. Homer's original verse was delivered in oral format, passed down from performer to performer. The five beat iambic pentameter, delivered with such skill by Chambers in this masterly and utterly compelling translation, retains that storytelling immediacy and energy.

These powerful and elegant sonnets are a poetic tour de force. Chambers' work is unique; the first time in Irish literature that such an ambitious undertaking has been attempted and it has been done with astonishing success.

The Odyssey is a tale of loyalty and betrayal; of caution, guile and stupidity; of honour and greed. Homer's brilliantly crafted story is fresh, using supposedly modern techniques such as flashbacks and split narrators.

The hero of the story, Odysseus, is a flawed but magnificent hero. He is described as polytropus. This may be translated as many sided or complex. Throughout the book Odysseus displays this characteristic again and again as he confronts the many obstacles and dangers on his ten-year journey home. He has been called the man of a thousand faces. Odysseus is a husband who has not seen his wife for twenty years; a father who has missed his son's upbringing; a warrior hero whose war is over; a leader whose men all die; an adulterer who is the plaything of nymphs and goddesses and a son who has left his parents broken-hearted. He is a voyager, a pirate, an adventurer, and a refugee. Odysseus twists words and situations to his advantage, never losing sight of his own self-interest. He is brave in battle but more often succeeds through cunning. He is also a consummate confidence trickster, the most skilful liar in literature!

Time and time again, what saves Odysseus is his mind. What gets him into trouble is his mouth!

The Odyssey charts the ten-year return journey taken by Odysseus [hero of the decade long Trojan War] and his crew to their homeland, Ithaca.

Behind him he has left his loyal wife, Penelope and a new-born son, Telemachus.

In his absence, a rough crowd of young men has occupied Odysseus' palace, raiding his livestock, and feasting off his food and wine. They put pressure on Penelope to marry one of them, telling her that her husband must be long dead. Penelope, mirroring her husband's caution and cunning, has managed to keep them at bay over several long, lonely years.

Telemachus, frustrated by this tense situation as well as by his inexperience and inability to expel the suitors, leaves to seek news of his missing father. He is helped by Athena, goddess of wisdom, who also champions his father.

Odysseus, meanwhile, after many setbacks, makes his way to his homeland, disguised as a beggar. There, with his son, he plots revenge on the young men who have abused his wife and his hospitality while he has been away.

Following a series of tests devised by Penelope, husband and wife are reunited.

Crucial themes in The Odyssey include the idea of nostos [the longing for home] and xenia [hospitality].

The action of this story is set against a backdrop of intervention by the family of gods. Zeus, Poseidon, Athena, Helios, Hermes, and other gods interfere in the world of mortals as they look down from Mount Olympus.

In the Odyssey, we see that Poseidon [god of the sea] sets out to destroy Odysseus as does Helios [god of the sun] while other members of the family of gods such as Athena [goddess of wisdom] and Hermes [god of travellers and messenger of the gods] try to help him on his long and challenging journey home to Ithaca.

John Chambers' stunning verse adaptation is loyal to Homer's epic and at the same time absolutely original. It is just over a century since James Joyce, published Ulysses, also based on The Odyssey. Now another Irish writer brings this timeless tale to life in our time.

Europe Books is proud to be on board this remarkable voyage.

Author's Foreword

I remember, at the age of ten, sitting ringside at a circus which had arrived at my hometown of Castlebar, in the west of Ireland.

The elephants, shuffling awkwardly on to metal stools, did not interest me. Neither did the well-fed, sleepy lions pawing lazily at the lion tamer, nor did the shouting clowns.

What held my attention was a tiger in a cage - too dangerous by far to be let out, the ring master announced!

Something about that trapped ferocity, that caged, pent up energy had me spellbound.

Writing a sonnet brings that memory to mind. The format is a tight cage of 14 lines, with 10 syllables as well as 5 beats in each one [iambic pentameter]

You are also faced with a strict rhyming scheme, building up to a clinching couplet at the end. All of this is just the cage. Unless you have that energy, restless for release, you only have technique.

Of course, the challenge level rises when you undertake to tackle one of the world's most significant literary works and try to rewrite Homer's epic entirely in sonnet form. The Odyssey, composed almost three thousand years ago, is the well spring of western literature. It is the standard bearer for every genre of storytelling-travel, romance, thriller, espionage, horror, comedy and science fiction.

I chose the 5 beat iambic line [the closest to that of everyday conversation] to retain a storytelling immediacy and have tried to steer this amazing narrative using language that is clear and precise while at the same time staying faithful to Homer's original work.

Now in our own time, let this tale be heard.

John Chambers

Proem: Introduction

Inspire me Muse, and let me tell the tale
of that cunning man, crafty to the core
who, after toppling mighty Troy set sail
with all his crew, bound for his native shore.
Wandering for many years on end,
he saw strange countries and observed the ways
of races that he met on sea and land.
On his journey, his steering hope always
was to save his own life and his shipmates too.
But despite his efforts, he was to see
the last surviving members of his crew
die by drowning – the price of gluttony
for killing and then eating the sun god's herd.
Now, in our own time, let this tale be heard.

A goddess intervenes

So, guide me Muse, and lead me to narrate
how Odysseus, spun out from travelling,
pining for his wife at home, was by fate
and the seagod Poseidon's tinkering,
knocked off course down south-eventually
washed up on Calypso's dreamy island.
This enchanting nymph's hospitality
kindled from kind welcome, like embers fanned,
into obsession's all consuming flame.
She clung to him; all her seductive skills
were so well used that he, who made his name
from cunning and wearing down of others' wills,
was like one drugged in body, mind and heart:
a man mismatched against immortal art.

Meanwhile the gods assemble to discuss
their own affairs and those of mortals too
in the hall of Zeus, on high Olympus.
There the grey eyed goddess Athena drew
her father aside and spoke her mind.
"A grievance done now needs to be undone
regarding Odysseus. Long years he's pined
for Ithaca, his homeland, his wife, his son.
Your brother Poseidon who rules the seas,
has stirred up storms to throw him off his course
through spiteful cold revenge. You have the keys
to make right this ongoing wrong. Ask, or force
your brother to turn rage and spite aside:
let this man home, with helping wind and tide"

"Daughter! This dispute is not a new one;
rooted in revenge on my brother's part
for a dreadful injury that has been done
by Odysseus-whose guile sets him apart
from all mortals. You know the story well:
One-eyed Polyphemus, slow of mind,
outwitted first, then left to painful hell
by Odysseus' cruel trick which left him blind;
that sharpened stake made red hot in a fire
poked through his one eye 'till it smoked and burst.
This savage outrage drew Poseidon's ire.
Right from the start my brother had a thirst
for bedding sea nymphs; one such fling
produced Polyphemus: revenge is the thing!"

There was silence, then great Zeus spoke once more.
"My brother has set lures as well as gales
in place to stop Odysseus touching shore
on Ithaca. Wherever brute force fails
he uses other tricks to gain his ends.
Right now, Odysseus lives as in a trance
on an island. A pretty sea nymph tends
to his every need, soft love, song and dance,
but all the while this poor man dreams of home.
Daughter, you are right! It is time for peace.
I'll send a messenger across the foam
and tell this brazen temptress to release
this weary wanderer who's paid his due.
I'll sort it all out with my brother too".

The grey eyed goddess Athena smiled and said
"Father, leader of all gods, of all men
who walk the earth below, of all the dead
who throng the underworld's gloomy cavern,
your wisdom is respected everywhere.
I will head to Ithaca, wing my way,
meet Odysseus' family-all trapped there
by packs of suitors, sniffing easy prey.
They tell Telemachus [Odysseus' son]
his mother must know her husband's dead for years
and press nightly marriage claims, one by one,
on Penelope. I'll soothe this young man's ears
with hope, encourage him to overturn
this gang, knowing his father will return".

And so, without delay, she bends to lace
her golden sandals, that speed her silently,
unseen by men, through the sky's airy space,
over the earth's green land and rolling sea.
She takes her own bronze bladed spear in hand
from a rack of weapons, then lifts for flight,
flashing and swooping - a comet brand
out of high Olympus - this wondrous sight
seen only by the gods. In one heartbeat
she stands in Ithaca's high-ceilinged court
where the suitors, gorged on fine wine and meat
have made themselves at home, and make rude sport
of Odysseus' servants. Pale, without a word,
his own son stands watching them, ignored.

Athena, changing form, stands in disguise
inside the entrance of that raucous place
as a young fisherman. The troubled eyes
of Telemachus rests on this new face
among the throng that's causing him distress.
He moves to greet the stranger with warm words
and stores the bronze bladed spear in a press
with his own long lost father's spears and swords.
He then brings his visitor from the din
and bustle of the dining hall to where
they might talk in peace, a side room within:
beckons his steward to bring fine wine there,
silver finger bowls, cuts of choicest meat,
a foot stool is placed under the traveller's feet.

"Dear guest, I hope that you will understand
why I moved you from these unruly swine
who foul my home. I, Telemachus, stand
helpless in my own hall. Vengeance would be mine
if my father could be restored to life.
Then I could join with him to put to flight
these animals, with spear and sword and knife.
Enough of that! I welcome you tonight.
What is your name? What brings you to this place?
One last question I ask each traveller
who visits here - I seek the slightest trace
of great Odysseus, my long lost father.
Have you news that we can mourn his death
or by chance report that he still draws breath?"

The goddess answered. "I sailed here with my crew
from Taphos, far across the winedark sea.
My name is Mentes. Ithaca is new
to me but before my birth my family
and yours were two ropes knotted as if one
[though loosening years have left those bonds untied]
I heard reports your father was due home
after years wandering the ocean wide.
To check the truth of these, I ventured here.
I see he's not arrived, he's been delayed,
but surely will turn up-you must not fear.
The sea can slow down man's quick plans: my trade
has been capsized by her whims, but I know
he is on his way here. Time will show".

Athena spoke again, still in disguise,
sensing that all her words were nectar sweet,
kindling hope and joy in this young man's eyes.
"Trust my word on this, shortly you will meet
your long departed father. Seek advice
from those you trust around you what to do
with these uninvited guests in your house;
for when, not if, your father comes they'll rue
the day they came to Ithaca's fair shore.
Unless they leave here soon, I can foresee
butchery here and bodies by the score".
As she spoke her face lit with prophecy
so that Telemachus, reading the sign,
knew this was no mortal guest, but divine.

She left him there, dazzled by the light
blazing from her figure and her face.
Outside the room, she laced her sandals tight,
took her bronze bladed spear down from its place
among the racked up weapons on the wall;
then tensed for flight, and lifted, and was gone
with no one knowing in that noise filled hall.
The goddess departed, her mission done,
leaving Telemachus quiet and wide-eyed
for some moments before he made his way,
seeking his mother who seldom strayed outside
her own bedroom door, mourning night and day
her lost husband. Her nature was too proud
to mingle with the loud and loutish crowd.

Meanwhile the suitors gorged on this night's feast,
gulped finest wine with feet stretched out on chairs,
roaring the coarsest songs. This din increased
until the racket could be heard upstairs.
Telemachus descended [he had found
his mother, her cheeks wet with tears, asleep]
strode among the rabble and stopped to pound
his fist three time against a beam. A deep
silence fell as each diner looked his way.
The young man spoke. "This is your final night.
Go feasting elsewhere! One more thing I'll say:
either depart from here by the morning's light
or else be well prepared for blood to spill.
This is my advice. Take it as you will."

The silence in the hall abruptly broke
when he had done, all clamorous again
with angry mutterings. Antinous spoke,
his voice moving from anger to disdain.
"Your high, mighty manner is quite strange;
a cloak you've just thrown on that's not your size.
I pray the gods above will not arrange
that you be master here and hope the prize
will fall to me or to a rival's claim".
With voice pitched strong and calm, Telemachus said,
"I would drag low my absent father's name
to leave his household as it's being bled
by leeches such as you. So, from tonight
I am lord of Ithaca, my birthright".

Eurymachus, Polybus' son, replied.
"It's in the god's gift who will rule this land
news of your father's fate they choose to hide
for reasons mortals cannot understand.
But I won't tempt their rage, won't linger here
if I am asked to leave-and that's your right.
By morning tide my crew and I will steer
for home. But let me ask, can you throw light
on the silent stranger's identity?
Where did he come from? Has he any news
of your father Odysseus, drowned at sea
or buried underground? The gods will choose
a man's final resting place when life is done;
when the Fates cut through the threads they have spun".

Telemachus listened and then made reply
in words that showed he shared his father's art
of cunning and of careful mastery
of what lay in his mind and in his heart.
"I would not trust a message if one came,
about Odysseus being alive and well.
My father is dead and gone. As for the name
of the guest that you inquire of, I can tell;
He is Mentes, his family and mine
are long connected". Telemachus knew,
deep at heart, his visitor was divine
but kept this to himself. The roaring crew
resumed their sport but by morning light
had, as Telemachus urged, gone from sight.

Telemachus, abruptly tired, withdrew,
anxious to leave the din for peace and quiet.
He reached his room upstairs, trying to sift through
the night's events. He felt his hunch was right;
his visitor was not of mortal flesh.
Eurycleia, his nurse from infancy
was there. She had laid silk sheets, cool and fresh
upon his inlaid bed and silently
picked up the tunic he'd thrown on the floor,
folded the garment, hung it in its place.
As he sat in thought, she clicked shut the door
gently behind her. Wrapped in finest fleece
he pondered on the road that lay ahead
for hours before he lay down on his bed.

The Debate

With the pale glimmering of dawn he woke,
his body and his mind refreshed by sleep;
drew on his tunic first and then his cloak,
then laced fine rawhide sandals to his feet.
He seemed transformed and those who knew him well
stopped and stared as he strode into the hall,
controlled and calm. He struck the summons bell
with a silver gong, an echoing call
to those who heard to come with urgency
and gather in the court's assembly place.
When all were there and waiting patiently,
he stood before them. At his heels a brace
of muzzled hounds and in his hands a spear:
he took his father's seat, no fuss or fear.

Lord Aegyptius, wise but of feeble frame,
opened the assembly. His son had been
a spearman with Odysseus, had made his name
in the siege and sack of Troy; his death obscene,
eaten by the brute Cyclops in his cave:
the final man of twelve to die that way.
The old man had three other sons but gave
way to loud weeping spells or quiet dismay,
mourning his absent one, that awful fate.
Slowly he stood, addressed those in the hall.
"Ithaca, who asked us to congregate
in full assembly here? You may recall
no meeting has been held here since the year
Odysseus was our king. Who called us here?"

Telemachus stood up and left his place
to grip the speaker's staff and faced the crowd,
pausing for a moment to embrace
the old man. When he spoke his voice was loud
and firm: the great hall became an ear.
"I called this meeting. It's my last resort.
My father is so long gone that I fear
he's gone for good. Ithaca's peaceful court
has been torn apart by upstarts who prey
upon your own first lady, to your shame!
I have urged these suitors to stay away
before they eat us out of house and home.
I've done that with no help from you at all".
In rage he threw the staff against the wall.

Touched by his anger, born of deep distress,
most stood still but for Antinous who said
"Nonsense Telemachus! Why not confess;
the cause of this lies at your mother's head?
For three years now she has been breaking hearts;
first leading on one man, then the next
on the side, then a third, with her soft arts.
Such tricks too! One that had us all perplexed:
she pledged that she would make a choice of one
among our group if given time to weave
a cloak. But work done by day was undone
by night, a sweet faced woman can deceive;
and we were fooled like this for three long years
until her maid brought her trick to our ears."

"Now hear this from us suitors, mark it well.
Dismiss your mother, send her from this place
or else force her to choose, and make her tell
which of us she will marry to our face.
She may be clever, have fine weaving skill;
but remember, as long as she holds out
this siege of ours goes on, goes on until
she surrenders and trust me there is no doubt
she will give in. Your little speech last night
and your cry for sympathy here today
won't put us off the track we know is right.
We've pitched camp here and here we mean to stay
until your mother accepts a wedding ring
from one of us and does the proper thing".

Telemachus listened and then replied,
"Curse the son who would do as you suggest
to his own mother, casting her aside.
Surely the gods will judge us on a test
of how we cherish those, who from our birth,
ensured through constant love and sacrifice
that we prosper. That test will show our worth.
So, I will pay no heed to your advice,
but ask again that you and all your friends
leave in peace my mother Penelope.
Do it straight away, before this ends
in doom, for Zeus will hurl, you will see,
his thunderbolts no mortal can withstand.
Leave Ithaca and do not force his hand!"

Now Zeus on high, listening to these words,
launched a pair of eagles in gliding flight,
wing tip to wing tip, guiding these great birds
from their mountain sanctuary into sight,
'till they poised above those assembled there.
They angled first, then swooped down from on high
on the uptilted faces, marked with fear.
Their talons raked at forehead, cheek and eye
then veered away above the city wall,
leaving uproar, confusion in their wake.
All standing there in that astonished hall
knew that this omen was one that they should take
as a warning sign that a stern god sent
as prophecy. This was no accident.

Old Lord Halitherses, well versed in skill
of translating birdflight [he was a seer]
addressed the crowd who stood there stunned and still
in quiet tones. "Those of you assembled here
remember years ago, that I foretold
Odysseus would return in twenty years,
unrecognised by all those in his household.
With these two great eagles a mystery clears;
I see him in my mind's eye on his way
to deal these suitors with raw bloody death.
My advice is to leave here while you may.
This is the time when you can still draw breath.
Heed my warning, leave through the palace gate
while there's a chance, before it is too late."

Eurymachus replied then with a sneer,
"Be quiet, old man! Great age has dulled your brain.
We're not like children to quake with fear
at daft talk of omens. Let me explain:
Odysseus won't come back. The man is dead
[a fate that might be yours before too long
if you stir up more trouble here.] You've said
the strangest thing and what you've said is wrong.
Telemachus should do as we say
and send his mother to her father's court,
arrange her wedding dowry straightaway.
Until he does that, courtship is our sport.
We don't intend to move out of this place
'till one of us wins this long distance race."

Telemachus stared at him and then replied
"Since my appeal is sown on barren ground,
I'll sail from Ithaca at the next tide,
and head for Pylos. There I'll search around
for news of my father, alive or dead;
tavern rumours or some traveller's tale.
If he's alive I will hold my head
until next year, return home under sail
with him to sort out all this madness here.
If he's dead, I'll come home straight away
to raise his funeral pyre and burn his gear
to honour a great hero passed away,
then let my mother choose a suitor's hand
when she's had chance to grieve her dead husband."

The veteran, Mentor, spoke up next, a friend
of Odysseus through several shared campaigns.
"What sickens me is how we did not send
this rabble on their way! Their presence stains
our honour. We're a laughing stock to all."
He went on like this but was forced to stop,
being shouted down by many in the hall.
In the end it was agreed that a ship
be fitted out and sail within a day
with Telemachus choosing his own crew
of twenty oarsmen. These he pledged to pay
wages in advance and a bonus too
for any man who had real news to tell
that Odysseus was still alive and well.

When this had been discussed the company
dispersed. Under the sun's white midday glare
Telemachus walked alone to the sea,
crouched at the slapping waves and said this prayer.
"Oh God, who met me yesterday
disguised as a guest; who bid me sail
in search of my lost father, I beg you to stay
with me. The suitors hope that I will fail,
my people have lost heart and will not rise
against those upstarts. My heart is sore"
Athena heard him cry and in disguise
[this time as Mentor] stood there on the shore.
The young man smiled, stood up and turned to face
his father's trusted friend: the two embrace.

Athena spoke in Mentor's kindly tone,
"Telemachus, it's time to show your will.
Know first of all that you are not alone.
I will muster up a crew, men of skill
with oar and sail then rig a sturdy ship.
You return home, let the suitors think
you've changed your mind and won't leave on this trip,
but on the quiet provision food and drink.
Make sure you have barley meal put by
[the food of oarsmen]. Store this watertight
in skin bags. Then a plentiful supply
of blood red wine from Ithaca corked tight
in amphorae. When this is all complete
and when I have a ship and crew, we'll meet"

Telemachus retraced his steps to where
the suitors at open fires were roasting meat,
carousing loudly in the courtyard square.
Antinous spotted him and stood to greet
him with these sly and insolent words.
"Telemachus, it's time to put aside
your anger here, it's no match for our swords.
We will help you sail on the morning's tide,
but for now, sit and drink good wine with us;
the way you used to do. What's done is done.
Believe me, we don't want to stir up fuss;
our lives are brief-set lengths that have been spun
by the fates-so each moment should be spent
avoiding care and seeking merriment."

Telemachus pushed the outstretched hand aside,
then standing at full height made this reply.
"Your presence is an insult to my pride.
If I had a ship and crew standing by,
I'd leave this place, although it is my home
and one day bring back doom upon your head.
But it suits you well I am quite alone
and forced to stay and suffer you instead".
Hearing himself, it seemed his father's guile
was now his own to use; dropped in his path
that art of disarming foes with a smile,
and then, in time, dispensing bloody death
He moved away. Meanwhile, stalling in flight,
two eagles poised overhead, out of sight.

From this place Telemachus went indoors,
descending steep steps to the family vault
holding gold and bronze alongside high shelved stores
of fragrant oil, of spices and of salt,
with mellow wine cool in high standing jars
kept for the day Odysseus would come home.
The place was kept secure by locks and bars;
keys kept by Eurycleia alone,
an old retainer of the family
who loved Telemachus as her own son.
He beckoned her to go and get her key
and open up the vault. When this was done
they stood together in the silence there;
breathing in the quietness, the cool still air.

"Nurse! This must be quietly done and in haste.
Take out twelve amphorae [first seal them tight]
of wine, not the one with vintage taste;
that one we keep to savour on the night
our lord Odysseus has returned to us.
Then fill out bags of barley meal ground fine.
Let no one know and see you make no fuss.
I will return to bring the food and wine
down to a ship that is being rigged to sail."
His loving nurse, tears welling in her eyes,
begged him to stay at home, to no avail.
At last, they both agreed that the supplies
would be stored where no one else might see
for Telemachus knew surprise was key.

Meanwhile grey eyed Athena, this time disguised
as Telemachus, was picking out a crew.
Not one of those selected realised
just who it was he had been talking to.
A ship was sourced, lent by Phronius' son
and the crew boarded her as darkness fell.
Athena passed, unseen by anyone,
among the revelling suitors; cast a spell
of drowsiness on them. They could not drink
another drop but reeled into the night
to heavy sleep. Athena, in a blink,
changed form again-stooped, hair snow white
as Mentor, stood at Telemachus' side
brought him to the ship, waiting on the tide.

They reached the water's edge where they could see,
moored at the pier, the rigged and ready ship.
Telemachus addressed his crew from the quay,
"My brave comrades, the rations for our trip
are stored, their location only known
by one true servant. I haven't even told
my own mother who will be left alone
against these suitors. But I know she'll hold
her own, keep their advances well in check".
He turned and led the way. The crew transferred
the stored supplies and lifted them on deck.
The young man boarded without another word;
goddess Athena, artfully disguised,
stood by him, completely unrecognised.

As a crewman untied the mooring rope,
Athena stirred up a quickening gust.
Seeing this, his heart swelling out with hope,
Telemachus ordered the tall fir mast
to be raised with great care, set amidship
inside its box. They fastened the forestays
then hoisted the sails. These began to whip
and billow with wind as they sailed away.
White flushing waves streamed backwards as they sped
towards open seas with dark land in their wake
and guided by the bright stars overhead.
Duties done; the crew assembled to make
libation to the gods and drank a toast
as the black ship moved southwards from the coast.

At the Court of Nestor

They sailed throughout the night or switched to oar
when winds dropped off, arriving at sunrise
outside Pylos town. On its sandy shore
they saw black bulls being led to sacrifice
in honour of Poseidon, lord of the sea.
There a multitude gathered round the pyre
and soon those watching from the deck could see
and smell the beef cuts skewering on the fire.
Telemachus seemed reluctant to leave ship
but Athena, seeing this, urged him on.
"You must not let presented chances slip
your reach. Explain you are Odysseus' son
seeking any scrap of news, any clue
of your long-lost father. This you must do".

Athena continued with her kind advice;
"Seek out old Nestor, master charioteer.
Ask him courteously - and that should suffice
for him to tell you all you need to hear.
He was your father's right hand man and friend."
Telemachus listened first and then replied
"Mentor, I'm too young and might offend
that grand old man. I haven't learned to hide
what's closest to my heart in proper speech
and I am just a stranger in this place".
Athena replied, "Join them on the beach.
Reason and heart and courage will all grace
your every word, and trust me when I say:
I know the gods will stand with you this day."

Telemachus ordered all the crew ashore
and as their group approached across the strand,
relieved to be on solid ground, a roar
of welcome rose to greet the weary band.
Peisistratus, Nestor's son, met them first,
beckoned them over to the royal tent
to pray, to share food and to slake their thirst.
There, among his family, frail and bent
with long years, Nestor bid them sit and rest
on soft lambskins and called for food and wine.
Silver water bowls were brought to each guest
to refresh hands and faces smeared by brine.
When wine was poured for each one present there
Peisistratus led them all in prayer.

Peisistratus stood up and then addressed
old Mentor [for little did he know
that the goddess Athena was his guest]
then passed the cup to her and bowed down low.
"Friend, I request you now to lead our prayer
to Poseidon. This is our ceremony
kept in his honour. This done, you may share
the goblet with your friend who we can see
sailed here with you into our port today.
He's young like me, your age commands respect;
so, I chose you to take this and to pray
to the great sea god. Then you may direct
your friend to take the wine and do the same;
invoking the god by his proper name".

He passed the goblet, returning to his place
and Athena smiled, liking this courtesy
that gave her precedence, this young man's grace.
She stood up now, addressed the company.
"We give praise to Poseidon, ocean king
with offerings of food and ruby wine.
May he bless those who ask with everything
their hearts desire; may their actions shine
with bright truthfulness and good intent
Keep Nestor and his sons safe in your care
and harbour those who gather in this tent.
For my young friend I offer one more prayer;
that by your great power we may be led
to find a long-lost leader, alive or dead."

Telemachus followed when she had done,
tipping his wine after his prayer was said.
Then food and drink was brought to everyone;
the beef, hot off the skewers, served with bread.
After the meal, old Nestor stood to speak,
"Welcome guests - it is time for us to ask
your names, your homeland. Who is it that you seek?
Is this visit by chance or does your task
involve us here? If so, what can we do?
I was a charioteer long years ago
and see how timely questions can push through,
can act like whip or spur when horses slow.
A question in its right place is an art
that speeds us on to what lies in the heart."

Telemachus spoke when Nestor was done.
"Your name is on men's lips far from this place;
Mine, as yet not known to anyone
outside of Ithaca which is my birthplace.
My father, Odysseus, who was your friend,
has not been seen since he sailed from Troy,
after that storied siege came to an end
through a wooden horse, his own clever ploy!
The mission that steers us here today
is to seek news of him, alive or dead.
Our hope is a fragile candle flame at prey
to every breeze; yet it lights our way ahead.
If you have word of one you once held dear,
I, his son Telemachus, am all ear"

Hearing this, Nestor, wide eyed with surprise
held Telemachus in a long embrace.
"My boy," he said "you have your father's eyes
and build and your voice echoes his dear voice.
We fought together to the bloody end
of Troy's long siege; that ten year old campaign
where countless fell, leaves torn to earth by wind.
Recalling great names lost, proud heroes slain,
Ajax, Achilles, Patrocles - each one
brings hard memories and such aching loss
that deepens as my dwindling life years run
me quickly to my death when I will cross
in Charon's boat to land on that black shore
and meet as shades my comrades there once more."

"Enough of this! Your mission is concerned
with your father that strategist of renown.
It was through his guile Troy was overturned;
its fabled topless towers brought crashing down.
When the fighting finished our ships raised sails,
but Zeus, furious at how Troy was lost,
shook our homeward fleet with howling gales
and mast high banks of rolling waves that tossed
our sturdy craft as if she was a toy.
Ships went down, ships scattered, ships ran aground,
some ships were even driven back to Troy!
We limped home. Since that time no sight or sound
of Odysseus, just rumours that disappear
like drifting smoke. You'll find no answer here."

Nestor continued. "A cause of grief and rage;
dark tales from Ithaca have reached our ears.
Your own mother trapped, songbird in a cage,
by uninvited suitors. It appears
this rough crowd have been granted bed and board!
Do your own people back them or back you?
Some day they may be routed by the sword
should your father return out of the blue.
If grey eyed Athena was in your camp
as she helped your father time and time again
during the war, she would have moved to stamp
those vermin underfoot and clear the stain
of their presence from Ithaca's great hall.
Where are the gods when the afflicted call?"

"As I speak, I sense your anxiety
to raise anchor on your quest and leave this place.
But hear me out before you put to sea.
If wisdom is an old man's saving grace
to compensate for time's relentless march,
then let this advice profit both of us.
There is one man whose council you should search.
If anyone can help Lord Menelaus
is that man! He has travelled far and wide
after the war and now is home again.
I will send you to him, with my own guide,
with chariots and horses and will rein
my own dear son to join you on your way.
Menelaus will help you. Make no delay!"

As Nestor talked the sun slipped down the sky.
Seeing this, Telemachus turned to go,
anxious to leave now out of loyalty
to his waiting crew on board and let them know
his plan to visit Menelaus next day.
But Nestor stopped him as he left and said
"No son of Odysseus who comes this way
will lie with hard deck timber for his bed.
You are my honoured guests in this house"
Grey eyed Athena, still in her disguise
as faithful Mentor, replied. "That makes sense
for my young friend to do as you advise:
there is much to discuss between you two,
but I will go on board, rejoin the crew."

Athena explained "Our ship's company
is young. I am, by far, the most senior there
and so must take responsibility
to keep their spirits up. I must take care
of old debts owed to me and settle scores
with the Cauconians the following day
and so may leave those young men to their oars
without my hand to guide them on their way."
As she spoke, Athena, in full sight
of all those watching, suddenly changed her shape,
this time a seahawk; lifted into flight
with a clap of wings, leaving them all to gape
upwards as the great creature wheeled and veered
across the darkening sky then disappeared.

Awed by what his eyes had seen, Nestor said
"My boy, it seems a god is on your side.
Could it be Athena? That goddess led
your father safely through where countless died
in Troy's long siege. She now is helping you
O Lady hear me! I will offer gold
and fine heifers - such are the honours due
the daughter of Zeus. This day I will hold
as sacred until death will seal my eyes."
He finished and Athena heard his prayer.
She had returned to ship, was in disguise
once more as Mentor, the crew unaware.
Meanwhile Telemachus as honoured guest,
was shown a royal bed and took his rest.

When dawn unfurled its pale rose-coloured light,
Lord Nestor made arrangements for the day,
sending out his eldest son to invite
Telemachus' crew, berthed in the bay;
another to the master of the herd
so that a prime heifer could be set aside
for slaughter. He sent one more son, his third
to tell the smith to bring his tools of trade
to glove each horn in foil of purest gold.
Then all the servants were assembled there
and the steward addressed them. Each one was told
what duties were required and each one's care;
seating, food and wine, fuel of seasoned wood.
The steward checked their work; found all was good.

At noon the smith, following Nestor's sign,
lifted the molten gold out of the flame
with tongs, then hammered it out wafer thin
to glove the horns. Then, in Athena's name
Nestor intoned the sacrificial prayer
before Thrasymêdês, expert with blade
sliced through the heifer's throat from ear to ear.
The black blood gushed in beating spurts then sprayed
into the sacred bowl. The choicest meat
was cut and burned for Athena the divine,
then all the company sat down to eat
the other portions from the spit. Rich wine
was served in bowls by the servants who stood
attentive to requests for extra food.

Later two mares were readied for the trip
then hitched to Nestor's gold-leaved chariot.
Telemachus stood and took the reins in grip,
Peisistratus at his side. At a trot
they left the waving crew and family,
Then, at a flick of Telemachus' rein
they were away from there. Soon few could see
their dwindling forms as they raced across the plain.
Within a heartbeat they were out of sight
to all those watching from the parting place
hands raised to shield the sun's hot midday light
that was dazzling every upturned face.
The crew then bid farewell and made their way
from Nestor's court to the boat without delay.

The two men, side by side, rode through the day
with each one taking turn to take the reins;
changing places at stops along the way.
Standing behind the horses' streaming manes
they talked, as young men of their age will do
of girls and games, of family gatherings
of matters serious and foolish too;
the only other sounds were the jingling
of the harness, their horses' drumming feet.
By the time they reached Pherae at sunset
to rest, to get fresh horses and to eat
they each realised a friendship had been set
as strong as if it had been always there;
Strangers yesterday, now a bonded pair.

They rose and broke their fast at break of day
then hitched fresh horses to the chariot.
When this was done, they steered without delay
through the echoing entrance gates at full trot
then urged the team with touch of whip and rein
to full speed, racing through the countryside
past fields of cows, past fields of flowing grain
arriving when the dipping sun had died
in a pool of crimson at the world's end.
Telemachus discussed his ongoing quest
and shared his worries with his newfound friend.
Both men were tiring, both set to rest
when at last they reached Lacedaemon;
its tall towers silvered by a full white moon

Melenaus and Helen

Upon arrival the travellers were shown
the palace of Menelaus the great King,
a mansion on high ground above the town.
The place was crowded - a double wedding
had taken place that very afternoon
- a son and daughter of the family.
The guests were roaring out a wedding tune
while jugglers entertained the company
on a raised stage with somersault and spin.
Telemachus and Nestor's son arrived
at the gate and shouted above the din
asking entry. The guards went back inside
moved through the revelling hall where King and Queen,
Menelaus and Helen observed the scene.

The sentry Eteóneus advanced
then bent down towards the king with lip to ear
(such was the tumult as the revellers danced
and sang - the place a din of wedding cheer)
"Two young men, both strangers, are at the gate.
Shall we admit them or send them both away?"
Menelaus made reply, his tone irate
"Sailing from Troy, could we have made our way
home to this very gate without support
of strangers and their hospitality?"
Hearing this, the sentry left the court
ordered men to set the tired horses free
from harness, watered down the steaming mares
fed them wheat, led the two young men upstairs.

Before the two were granted audience
with King Menelaus they were brought inside
the bathing rooms where oil and sweet incense,
warm water and fresh tunics were supplied.
Soon they sat as two honoured guests on thrones
before the king as carvers heaped up meat
on plates before them; trays of loaves and scones
with local wine and both were urged to eat.
When they had done, red haired Menelaus said
"You are welcome here on this wedding day
and now that you are rested and have fed
let's hear your names and how you come this way.
If appearances can present a truth
it seems you are both well bred, not base youth."

"I see you looking round this splendid hall
luminous with amber, ivory, gold,
bronze and silver too. I would strip each wall
and tabletop and live in want and cold
if I could bring my brother from the dead.
Murdered in cold blood, arranged by his wife;
or if I could see again the noble head
of Odysseus, my comrade in that strife
which brought the great walls of Troy tumbling down.
No one took on as much, went through such woe
as brave Odysseus did. It is not known
what became of him. Only the gods know
if he's alive with each passing day
his wife and son can only hope and pray."

Hearing these things said, Telemachus cried,
holding his purple tunic to his eyes
to mask his grief. Menelaus realised
who was sitting there; was about to rise
to hold this sad young man in long embrace
when, out of private chambers to the rear
Queen Helen appeared with soft flowing grace
and she caught sight of Telemachus there.
"My lord, what is this sad eyed young man's name?"
And yet I have a feeling that I know
He and a long lost hero share the same
face and form. I feel it must be so
this is the child Odysseus left behind
to rescue me when lust had led me blind."

Then red haired Menelaus spoke once more
"My dear, I see the likeness as you do
and noticed he was grieving to the core
when I spoke of Odysseus going through
such hardship and such horrors those years at Troy."
Now Nestor's son spoke for his weeping friend
"Yes, this is brave Odysseus' only boy
we've been sent here by Nestor, your old friend
to seek advice. Ithaca is beset
by suitors who harass Odysseus' wife,
Penelope - they also are a threat
to Telemachus, plotting on his life
while he is away from home on the sea.
It is Telemachus who sits with me."

Queen Helen replied. "On this wedding night
you two are welcome as if family.
Odysseus was a man of keen insight.
Permit me to look back in memory,
recalling something that he dared to do.
He dressed as a beggar by Troy's high wall,
then gave himself a beating, then slipped through
the guarded gates, unrecognised by all,
except for me. I knew him straight away
and questioned him but he gave me no news,
shrewdly putting me off, then made his way
safely outside again and by this ruse
learned about the city's defensive strengths
and then rejoined the Greeks in their siege tents."

Helen spoke again. "As I watched him leave
that night in Troy before the city fell,
hobbling through the streets, dirt on each sleeve,
I cursed my lot again and cursed the spell
that took me from my child, my husband's bed,
from my homeland to that accursed place.
Because of me so many men were dead.
Madness! From that night on I hid my face
from every mirror, every glass and pane
hating these features that launched a thousand ships
sailing out to that nine year long campaign.
From that night, as I watched a beggar slip
to my old friends, outside the walls of Troy
I knew, till I left there, I'd have no joy."

"I too" said Menelaus, "have never seen
a man to match Odysseus' cunning mind.
I remember hearing your voice, my queen
as we hid in the wooden horse designed
by that clever hero who realised
Troy's siege would end not through force but by guile.
You called us by our names, your voice disguised
to imitate our loved ones; all the while
circling the horse, patting it everywhere.
Inside its frame, each man longed to reply
when his name was called but each took care
to stay in hiding until you had walked by.
All but Anticlus who stood up to call;
Odysseus' great hand clamped his jaw saved us all."

Menelaus and Helen took turns that night
recounting deeds of guile and bravery
done by Odysseus. His son's eyes were bright
with tears prompted by each new memory.
Then Helen, seeing the two young men were tired
send servants with torches to light their way
upstairs to bed. King Menelaus retired
arm in arm with Helen without delay.
But he was first to wake and first to rise
and, when Telemachus had woken too,
sat by his side, looked deep into his eyes
and said "My boy, I need to hear from you
what mission takes you two days' riding here?
A public or a private cause? Let me hear."

"Lord Menelaus, I came to hear what news
you have of my father, your trusted friend.
I speak as one with everything to lose
- it seems as if my sorrows have no end,
with everything I hold dear under threat.
I see you are surprised. Let me narrate
my woes. Each day my mother is upset
by bullying suitors who congregate
in my father's great hall to court his wife.
They claim our wine supply and gorge our meat.
Another hurt that slices like a knife
through my heart is not knowing if I'll meet
my long lost father on this earth again.
If you know he's dead, don't spare me pain."

Menelaus said "A long lost memory
broke through the surface of my sleep last night.
After Troy, we were swept off course at sea,
pushed southwards to the Nile. There, in my plight
I asked the Ancient of the Sea for aid;
an oracle who haunts the ocean's floor.
I tracked him down and this is what he said.
My crew and I would reach our native shore
if due sacrifice to the gods was done.
I also asked him to tell me the fate
of good friends of mine on their homeward run
from the great war at Troy and will relate
his three reports. The first one of my crew
then my brother's fate and your father's too."

"The first one, Ajax, survived fierce storms at sea
then boasted he was safe despite Poseidon's will.
The great god punished this audacity
swung his mighty trident and split the hill
this proud fool stood on. It sank without a trace
into churning seas and Ajax was drowned.
As for my brother, he reached his own homeplace,
unscathed, but he learned familiar ground
can harbour horrors of the cruellest kind.
He was made welcome and later in the night
a meal was set before him. As he dined
he was hacked to death in his own wife's sight
by her lover. His crew, each one in his seat,
were butchered as they ate, like pigs for meat."

Through streaming tears, I asked the oracle
to let me know about Odysseus' fate.
The ancient answered "Now I will tell
you of Laertes' son, Odysseus the great.
I see him whitefaced, standing by the sea
that circles round the nymph Calypso's place
He looks a picture of sheer misery
Seduced by all her charms, her form, her face
he now regrets that he has shared her bed,
pines for a ship to take him far away
from an enchantment that has turned to dread.
Menelaus, I predict you'll find your way
home in safety with all your captured wealth.
You'll live to ripe old age in sturdy health."

Hearing this, Telemachus' spirits surged
a tidal wave of joy rose in his heart.
He left that day, though Menelaus urged
him and Peisistratus with such subtle art
and sheer persuasive charm that both should stay.
But Odysseus' young son would not agree,
anxious to return to Pylos without delay.
He was brimming with hope that he might see
his beloved father, alive and well.
And as he left, the young man was embraced
by Helen on whose behalf thousands fell
in war, leaving great Troy itself erased.
Telemachus mounted and took the rein;
the two men sped across the level plain.

Meanwhile, in Ithaca, the suitors spent
their days at discus, javelin, games of speed
on a measured field then lolling in a tent
when the sun was high. At night they would feed
and drink without restraint into the dawn.
One day, Noêmon, watching a javelin throw,
addressed the leader Antinous, with a groan.
"I lent my own ship five days ago
to Telemachus and need it straight away
to sail to Elis. I have brood mares there
with young mule colts. Without any more delay
I must round them up and sail back here
and break them in for labour and for sport.
I need a ship to sail to Elis port."

These words of Noêmon made the suitors stare.
They had been told the young man had left court
with friends, to savour the cool upland air
of Ithaca's pastures. This new report
worried them so they questioned Phronius' son.
"Who sailed with him? Tell the story true.
You say it was your boat - how was that done?
Did he take it, or did he come to you?"
"I lent it to him freely" Noêmon confessed
"He is my oldest friend, dear to my heart.
As for his crew, he chose the very best
to join him. But this is the strangest part
I noticed Mentor boarding as they set sail
yet he's here at court each day without fail."

The suitors listened, anger in their hearts
then Antinous addressed the hostile group.
"It could be human will or divine arts
that has let this chicken escape the coop.
How it happened is not today's concern.
We can nip this in the bud straight away;
let's rig a ship and crew it bow to stern
with trusted men, and sail from here today,
hold filled with water and with food supplies.
We'll head out to Samê, then lie in wait
and take this cocky bastard by surprise;
spring an ambush when he sails through the strait.
We'll kill our little chicken, slit his throat."
The suitors roared, then headed for the boat.

Medon, the crier, had been standing there
and so overheard their conspiracy.
He ran like the wind, desperate to share
the suitor's evil plan with Penelope.
She was sitting, a prisoner in her room.
When he entered, she looked up in dismay.
"Have they sent you here checking on my loom?
The day my weaving's finished is the day
I've pledged to receive offers for my hand
in marriage. But by night I have undone
each day's weaving and now they all demand
I finish off the work. I'd tell my son
but he is with his friends, at hunt, at sport
while I am hunted here in my own court."

"I wish that was the worst of it", Medon said
"But, my Lady, your son has sailed from here
for news of his father. The suitors head
up the coast to Samê. From what I hear
they mean to wait in ambush at that place
until his ship sails through that narrow strait
on its homeward voyage. There he will face
a savage end, tossed like discarded freight
into the sea. They'll kill him first on board
stabbing at him with spear and sword and knife."
Penelope tried to speak, but not a word
could she bring to her lips. Odysseus' wife
stood there stunned until Medon closed the door,
then turned and sank in tears upon the floor.

Soon servants ran in, hearing her wild cries
and her old nurse Eurycleia stroked her hair,
whispered to her, encouraged her to rise.
Penelope spoke "Surely someone here
knew of my son's intentions but kept it quiet
I could have acted if I had been told
and he'd be safe in Ithaca tonight!
The father left me, now I cannot hold
the son! Why has Zeus given me such pain?
Find a trustworthy runner to bring the news
to Laertes; Odysseus' father. His clear brain
belies his great age and he won't refuse
a mother's plea for help to save her son.
It's not too late - their plan can be undone."

With eyes downcast, Eurycleia replied
"My lady. Telemachus made me swear
to tell you nothing of his plans. I tried
to change his mind but patience is so rare
in youth. As we left our separate ways
he put me under oath not to pass on
his plans to anyone before twelve days
from our time of meeting had come and gone.
He feared that if by accident or fate
you heard of this before that time was through
your mother's heart would labour with the weight
of worry. If so, he asked me to ask you
to trust your son and seek Athena's care
through daily, intercessory prayer."

The old nurse stayed at Penelope's side,
soothing her with whisper and soft caress,
with oiled essences cunningly applied
and by and by encouraged her to dress,
then gently led her to the balcony.
Her mistress stood there; eyes closed tight to pray
to Athena. "Child of Zeus, hear my plea,
For long years now my lord has been away.
Many think I am a widow here
and now my son has slipped the ropes that moor
a mother to her child. Just now I hear
a team of killers will set sail to lure
him to his death. I beg the gods on high
to save a son and hear a mother's cry."

Meanwhile, gathered in the hall below,
the suitors drank, boasting what they would do.
Antinous cried "Fools! Keep your voices low.
We need to work this out and choose a crew,
stow food and drink on board and sail from here
and do all this in total secrecy."
They drained their drink and headed to the pier.
There a smaller group, experienced at sea
were chosen one by one. Later that night
all those who were selected slipped away
while all the revelling was in full flight,
down to the waiting ship moored in the bay.
The craft moved out of sight, left land behind
main sail billowing in a driving wind.

Penelope woke time and time again,
disturbed by dark nightmares that left her chill.
Grey eyed Athena moved to ease her pain
and fashioned a vision by divine will
to take the place of those tormenting dreams
of Iphthimê, a sister of Penelope
sent her gliding through the air like moon beams.
This image moved to the bed noiselessly
and murmured to the drowsing figure there
"Sleep well my sister. Ease your troubled mind.
All will be well. Athena will take care
to see your troubles lifted. You will find
your present sorrow turned to future bliss.
Your sister seals this promise with a kiss."

Penelope, half sleeping, now replied
"Sister, to see you here is wonderful,
our father must have urged you to my side;
knowing that my cup of sorrow is so full.
My stouthearted husband has gone long years
and now my son is sailing towards his doom,
leaving me a slave to fits and tears,
afraid to leave the confines of my room.
I'm told he will be ambushed while at sea
and die a violent death. All this planned
by those same suitors who imprison me.
Can you give me hope that Athena will stand
to protect my son from this looming snare;
will a great goddess heed a mother's prayer?"

Now the dim phantom spoke to her again
"Cast aside your worry and do not fear.
Pallas Athena listens to your pain
and pledging to give you hope sends me here
to assure you that she will save your son."
Penelope answered with a joyous face
"One last question to you, then I am done.
Oh tell me of Odysseus - does he pace
this mortal world of ours or does he tread
the dark halls of the dead? I have no leave
to tell you now if he's alive or dead."
Iphthimê said "I have no news to give."
The phantom turned and moved, melting from sight,
left the queen in calm sleep through the night

Calypso: The honey trap

On Olympus, Athena spoke her mind
"Father Zeus, Odysseus is still not free
from the nymph Calypso. He is confined,
a prisoner of her carnal artistry.
He lacks a ship or crew to sail away.
The seductive joys of Calypso's bed
drugs his mind but even in passion's play
he longs for Ithaca his home instead.
And now the suitors plan to kill his son
who has left home to track his father's fate.
We gods must see that justice is being done
and justice is injustice if done too late.
Let us act now and take the proper course
whether by guile, advice or show of force."

That great summoner of storms smiled and said
"All that you request, my child, will be done.
Odysseus will return. No need to dread
the trap those suitors prepare for his son.
He will be safe from harm. Now I will tell
Hermes, our messenger, to wing his way
to Calypso's cave and order that the spell
she has made must be unmade straight away.
We will give Odysseus a parting test.
Without a crew, let him build a raft
and lash it true and watertight to crest
the waves that he must face in that frail craft."
He turned to where his son was standing near
and whispered commands into Hermes' ear.

Hermes listened and then he stooped to tie
his golden sandals that propelled his way
through the world; like a hawk might fly,
veering in the air, skimming the sea spray.
In a heartbeat he had swooped low to land
at Calypso's cave. She was reclining there
on rugs beside a fire, wine glass in hand;
a drowsy smell of incense in the air.
A second glass stood on an alcoved shelf
by the hearth, ready for her captive mate.
Odysseus, meanwhile, had strayed off by himself
as was his habit, staying out 'till late,
facing the ocean, heart and mind both sore
to see his home and family once more.

Immortals know each other straight away
through an inner lens that fleshes the divine.
So, Calypso, rising from where she lay
recognised Hermes. She knew well that wine
was no fit drink so served her heavenly guest
with ambrosia and nectar on a tray.
She sat him down; he ate and drank with zest.
When he was done, he proceeded to relay
the message from mighty Zeus, word for word,
that Odysseus should now be free to go.
Calypso stood there, shocked by what she'd heard
her eyes sparkling with anger and with woe.
She knew that the will of Zeus had to stand
supreme. This was not request but command.

"Why is it that Zeus hates it when we lie
with mortal flesh? Could it be jealousy?
Zeus may have sunk his boat, but it was I
who saved Odysseus from the hungry sea.
I nursed and fed him, grew to love him too,
through divine, seductive skills made him mine.
But how can he leave here, without a crew,
without ship; now surely that's a sign
he should remain with me and warm my bed?"
Hermes answered her, anger in his voice
"You heard my message - it is on your head.
If you refuse to act, that is your choice
but if I were you, sweet nymph, I'd obey
this commandment. Odysseus must not stay."

Calypso, stirred by his words, moved to where
Odysseus sat, perched high above a beach,
alone and desolate, fixing his stare
across to Ithaca beyond his reach.
Day after day he'd sit, tears in his eyes
and yet at nightfall share Calypso's bed.
But even when in spasm between her thighs
he'd yearn for his waiting wife instead,
Calypso approached, stroking his red hair
and Odysseus turned, his face drawn and grey.
"My sad lover, I won't detain you here.
Hear me! You are released to go your way.
This is not my wish, let you have no doubt.
What Zeus has ordered, I must carry out."

"My lord, it's been decreed you should depart
my island home, my bed without delay
and leave me nothing but a shattered heart.
Zeus has planned it all, you must obey;
this is what you must do immediately.
You must lash hard planks to make a raft
and take your chances on the open sea
alone, captain and crew on that frail craft.
I will send you on your way with a store
of food and water and ruby coloured wine,
send you a wind to move you out from shore.
After that, it's the will of Zeus, not mine
if you are to sink or else reach home again.
Both options as I view them now bring pain."

"O sweetest nymph, what guile is hidden here?
A raft, you say! What use is that to me?
I need a ship and crew. How would I steer
a toy like that across the roaring sea?
But if this mad scheme is my only way
to reach Ithaca, I won't hesitate.
But swear this oath to me without delay
that when I leave this island place my fate
will be set free from your control, your spell."
Calypso smiled. "You are cunning to the end.
My hold on you is gone. I wish you well.
Whatever trials or tests the gods may send
will not unfold through me. You hold my heart
and hold it even if we have to part."

The nymph continued, "You would not leave my side
if you could see the dangers that await
you on the journey home and those that bide
to ambush you in Ithaca - you'd wait
with your loving Calypso here in bliss.
Can your wife be so beautiful, so wise,
is my kiss no match for Penelope's kiss?"
Odysseus said "Your beauty never dies
whereas age will mark my wife's mortal face
and yet it's her I long to hold so tight
even when I am deep in your embrace."
As they conversed, the day had ebbed to night.
They slept together by mutual desire
- one last log tossed on a dying fire.

At rose coloured dawn the following day
Odysseus and Calypso rose from sleep.
He with energy, she in quiet dismay
at losing something that she'd hoped to keep.
Nonetheless she brought him a bronze axe head,
two bladed, with a heft of olive wood
and a well polished adze. Then she led
the red haired hero to where tall pines stood.
He started chopping them and lopped and split,
then cut each plank and placed them side by side.
With the augur he drilled holes through and knit
the decking with willow strands securely tied.
He cut a mast pole and shaped out an oar,
then hauled his raft on rollers to the shore.

This all took four long days of sweat and craft,
of aching limbs, but in the end quiet pride
in knowing that he'd built a sturdy raft.
Calypso stitched a sail and this he tied
in place along the mast. On the fifth day
she bathed his tired body with soft care,
bringing her skills with healing oils to play,
then trimmed his beard and cut his wild red hair,
placed fresh clothes before him, new sandals too,
and set up stores of food and wine as well.
Watching him board, then slowly move from view
she sobbed. She knew this man she'd loved so well
who had been taken from her, ripped apart
would stay forever rooted in her heart.

Odysseus stepped on board and rowed away,
then shook out sail to catch Calypso's breeze.
He made good progress, stopping twice a day
to rest. The testing hardship of the seas
were relished by this master mariner
who kept the same routine throughout the night
reading the Great Bear, the Plough, the northern star
guiding his homeward path by their high light.
Odysseus sailed for seventeen long days
before his keen eye, hungry to see land
made out a shape emerging from sea haze.
It was Scherie, whose cliffs darkly stand
sheer and stern and high. Odysseus rowed ashore
anxious to walk on solid land once more.

Now Poseidon, observing from on high,
grew sullen, "My brother Zeus has lost his mind
to let Odysseus escape home safe and dry."
The sea god churned the deep, called up a wind
of fearsome force and waves of towering height
that reared and broke across the slender mast.
And now the midday sky turned black as night,
forked with lightning and loud with thunder blast,
Watching this hellish storm, Odysseus cried
"I well deserve a soldier's noble death
like all my friends who fought at Troy and died
not this choking, drowning fight for breath
in this unmarked lonely place, lost at sea
forever more. Is that my destiny?"

Just then a wall of water with toppling crest
broke on the raft and swept him overboard
oars wrenched from his grip. The wooden mast
was split in two by a twisting gale that roared
as if a savage beast was snarling there.
It ripped the sail and spun it out of sight.
Odysseus surfaced slowly, gulping air
with choking breath, then, with all his might
clung to the upturned mast and gripped the base
of the shattered mast with first one hand, then two.
Half drowned Odysseus held on in this place
somehow foiling death as Poseidon threw
a raging storm against him without check,
across the huddled figure on the deck.

Observing this from her deep sanctuary
below the waves, the undine Ino sped
and broke the surface of the turmoiled sea.
She was an immortal, a neriad,
a band of sea nymphs who strove to save
mariners from the fate all sailors fear.
In a heartbeat she rode a savage wave
on to the rocking raft and then moved near
to where Odysseus lay stretched out and spoke
"Poor man! I wonder why Poseidon bore
such grudge against you? You must shed your cloak
and leave your raft and swim towards the shore.
Take my veil. It's magical fabric saves
but once you reach dry land, cast it to the waves."

She gave her veil, then disappeared from sight,
leaving Odysseus perplexed on the boat
"Could this be a trick? Better to hold tight
while this battered planking keeps me afloat.
The coastline she talked of seems far away
so, I may well ride out this tempest here.
I cannot think this through a better way."
This being settled, he said a hurried prayer
that Athena would ensure he would not drown
with none to know his final resting place.
Then gripping Ino's veil, he huddled down
on the buckling deck, averting his face
from the force of water hurtling his way,
wondering if Athena had heard him pray.

Now as Odysseus planned this strategy
Poseidon sent a wave against him, sheer
as a rearing cliff, black as ebony
increasing in its pace as it drew near.
Just as piled chaff is scattered by a breeze
far and wide, so too this gigantic wave
smashed the raft's stout planks apart with ease.
Odysseus gripped a single beam to save
himself from drowning in the raging sea,
and like a jockey rode the moving plank.
He tore Calypso's cloak and tossed it free
and slung the veil of Ino round his neck
then plunged into the sea, his arms, and feet
lifting and kicking with a swimmer's beat.

Odysseus swam and floated on the swell
two days and nights. He felt his destiny
having first faced and then survived the hell
of shipwreck, would not let him drown at sea.
Riding a rolling wave at start of day
the third morning, he caught a glimpse of land.
This gave him heart. He started straight away
to swim for the coast, desperate to stand
on solid ground again. But drawing near
he heard the booming roar of sea on rock.
No caves, harbours or sandy beaches here
only sheer sharp headlands. No boat could dock
never mind a swimmer who needed rest.
He wondered how he'd pass this extra test.

Poseidon sent a massive surge, deep and high
that would have drowned Odysseus there and then
or flayed him off the rocks and bled him dry.
But this most brave, this wiliest of men
gripped a ledge as the water toppled near,
held on for dear life as it swept along.
Then the backwash hit him, pulling him clear.
It's said an octopus' grip is strong
and when dragged from its underwater lair
comes up with suckers full of tiny stones.
So, Odysseus left behind him there
the skin of his hands. Then with cries and groans
he found himself swept out to sea again,
his shredded fingers pulsing with the pain.

The backwash spewed Odysseus out to sea
and then, for once, good fortune took his side.
Struggling to breast the surface, he could see
a glimpse of shoreline, free from rocks and wide.
Praising Athena for coming to his aid
[for in his heart he sensed she'd steered him here]
he found an inner strength to swim and wade
on to the level shore and collapsed there
swollen and bleeding, bruised from foot to head,
seawater gushing from his mouth and nose.
He lay, barely breathing, as if half dead.
When he recovered breath Odysseus rose
and tossed Ino's veil. A hand, slender, white,
appeared out of the sea, pulled it from sight.

Princess Nausicaa

Odysseus, desperate to close his eyes
in sleep, moved up shore to a place of shade
under two olive trees, perfect for his size.
Here he tunnelled out a bed, having laid
one clump of fallen leaves to ease the base,
another as a pillow for his head
then one more pile around him to embrace
his cold body, then stretched out on his bed,
laughing, despite his battered, exhausted state
to see himself, a hero of renown,
like a creature about to hibernate.
And so, he laughed and lay his tired head down,
settling gently into his leafy heap.
Athena gifted him a deep long sleep.

Alcinous was king of the countryside
where Odysseus found shelter from the storm.
As he slept in his burrowed leafy hide
the goddess Athena altered her form
and stood at Alcinous' daughter's bed
disguised as the best friend of the princess.
She bent low to Nausicaa's ear and said
"Your wedding day draws near. Make sure each dress
you store in your wedding chest is washed clean.
You must tell your father when dawn comes round
to have the mule cart harnessed as you mean
to ride out to the washing pools and pound
your undergarments, gowns, linen and lace.
Tell him you'll bring a picnic to that place."

Athena now moved softly from the bed
and in a sudden stir of air was gone.
At dawn the princess rose; lodged in her head
Athena's words. Her father was alone
preparing for a council of the court.
Nausicaa approached him with her request
and soon the stable boy brought round the cart
with picnic provisions packed in a chest.
Her mother gave her jars of olive oil
to take along for all the company
to use while bathing after their toil.
The clothes for washing were stored separately.
Nausicaa took the reins and raised her whip;
The rest followed in convoy on the trip

At last, the wagons reached the washing place,
where clear waters cascade, bubble, spill.
Servants unhitched the mules and let them graze
sweet upland meadow grasses at their will,
then gathered the soiled clothing from the box
straight to the washing pools and trod them there
'till they were clean and spread them out on rocks
to dry under sunlight and upland air.
Now with duty done the fun began
they frolicked in the rippling water pool;
princess, friends, servants as one in their skin,
rubbed soft with oil, then lay out in the cool,
then dressed and then all settled down to feast;
all side by side, the greatest with the least.

When they had cleared the picnic things away
they played ball games in a flat and tree-lined place.
It happened that a ball was thrown astray
into the bobbing stream. A group gave chase
high shrieking as the ball moved towards the sea.
Odysseus, woke up from his leafy bed
and pushed aside the branches cautiously
and moved outside, leaves helmeting his head
his body swollen, bruised, congealed in blood
with only leaves to hide his nakedness.
He looked so terrible there as he stood
they turned and ran away in great distress.
Only Alcinous' daughter remained there
so bravely facing this half man, half bear.

Odysseus wondered what was best to do
to ensure this girl would not run away.
Soft tones might work, soft praise and pleading too.
"Lady, I am a wretched castaway
buffeted by tempests through day and night.
A commander of troops, now fallen low.
I beg you now to help me in my plight,
I sense your beauty is no outward show
but pointing to an equal grace within.
Fair princess - for I sense your family
is proud and high, let me cover my skin
with some clothes to protect my modesty
some linen from that laundry left to dry.
Earn this man's blessing and the gods on high."

"I've heard it said" Nausicaa answered back
"That Zeus can treat good men and bad as one
for reasons unknown to us. Mortals lack
divine understanding. What's done is done
and brave men bear their fate with grace and cheer.
Since I sense you are of noble learning
you will not lack a friendly welcome here.
We are Phaeacians. He who is our king
is my own father." Turning to the rest,
as they watched quietly from afar, she said
"This is no enemy, this is our guest
who is like one returning from the dead.
He needs clothing, drink and food to eat
a chance to bathe and sandals for his feet."

They led Odysseus to the washing place
and laid out everything on a rock beside:
jars of oil for his body and his face,
fresh towels too and clothing all supplied.
"Tall stranger, bathe in this clear pool." they said
but Odysseus answered them, "Leave me be
to wash brine from my body and my head.
I can't be naked in such company."
So, they left him to wash and wallow there
scrubbing a coat of salt from head to toe
He rubbed on oil and trimmed his russet hair
then dressed himself. Now he seemed to glow
with godlike grace, with godlike golden skin,
with a godlike beauty lit from within.

They watched in awe as he returned their way
this naked wretch transformed as if divine.
They placed before him on a silver tray
a tempting store of picnic food and wine,
and how this starving man wolfed down each bite
drained each long draught, nodding when offered more
until he'd satisfied his appetite.
Standing close to Odysseus to ensure
she was not overheard by friend or maid
Nausicaa said "Until we reach the town
stay beside me. From there I am afraid
of rumours that would make my father frown
that his one daughter, soon to be a bride,
was walking with a new man at her side."

She continued then, "At the city walls,
you'll find a roadside fork. There you can stay
in that cool shaded place 'till evening falls.
This plan will give me time to make my way.
When you imagine we're home safe and well
move through the city gates. Ask anyone
for the king's mansion [anyone will tell]
It's built on highest ground, of finest stone.
Go to the mégaron when you get there
where my mother and father sit at ease.
Approach my mother first and let her hear
your story up to now then clasp her knees.
If her heart is stirred by your grief and pain,
she'll help you find your own way home again."

The mules were harnessed for the homeward trip
with picnic things and laundry packed away.
The princess took her place and flicked her whip
and moved the straining team without delay
from a canter into a speedy trot
through woodland and through open countryside
until they had approached the roadside spot
beside the city walls where he could bide
his time until he judged the time was right
to travel to the palace of the king.
Odysseus dismounted, slipped out of sight
into the park as the loaded wagons swung
through the thick-walled city gates and then sped
towards home, sunset a glowing ball of red.

Before he left the park, Odysseus prayed
to Athena "I seek your help once more,
although it seems you gave me little aid
when I was storm battered and swept on shore.
May I find safety and warm welcome here,
after all my suffering on the sea."
Pallas Athena heard him [she was near
as his shadow was - not that he could see]
She heard all this, but out of deference
to her father's brother did not show
her feelings, not wanting to cause offence
among the gods above or men below.
The grey eyed goddess vowed to hide her hand
until Odysseus reached his own homeland.

The Palace of Alcinous

Odysseus, when the time agreed had passed
left the park for the palace of the king.
Athena helped him now as in the past,
and poured a fog around him, preventing
those at the city gates from catching sight
of a godlike stranger as he passed by.
As well as that, the goddess took delight
in changing shape again so to his eye
she was a little girl, absorbed in play.
Odysseus asked the child to be his guide
and bring him to the court without delay.
Looking up at him, Athena replied
"I will show you the way, just follow me."
She moved. Odysseus followed silently.

Athena ran ahead, setting the pace
and he followed, hidden from all men's eyes
by the screen of sacred fog she'd put in place.
And so, he moved, unhindered, in disguise.
Though concealed himself, he could look at will
marvelling at the ramparts, ships, and great square.
They soon approached the castle on the hill
and Pallas Athena said "We are here.
The king and queen are in the dining hall.
Go straight to Queen Arete. She is wise
and beautiful, much loved by one and all
for her good nature and her sound advice.
She will give you help if you ask her to."
The young girl turned, then disappeared from view.

Approaching the royal court, he could see
a splendid orchard, bordered by a fence.
Pears, figs and apples burdened every tree
vines and olives ripened there. A fragrance
of nature's bounty filled the evening air.
Currants dried on a platform at one end
facing the sun, and vats of grapes stood there
for pressing by the vitners. Near at hand
were vegetables in a separate place,
row after row, enough there to supply
the requirements of a bustling palace.
Fed by fountains and water tanks on high
a maze of channels let clear water course
to all the roots below and served the house.

Odysseus, left alone, stood lingering there
planning how best he might approach the queen.
At last, he strode across the entrance square
and passed the gate tower guards without being seen.
To the right and left of him he could see
reception rooms, ablaze with candlelight
where the cream of Phaeacian nobility
feasted. Odysseus marvelled at the sight
of such delicious and abundant fare
heaped high on silver trays, tall jugs of wine,
the stylish clothing of the people there,
with watchful servants waiting in a line,
high gold framed mirrors hanging on each wall:
Odysseus moved towards the royal hall.

At the door he paused, with wide open eyes
taking in the ordered opulence
of this splendid court; in wealth and size
a match for Ithaca. He had a sense
from looking at the people passing by
servants, soldiers, court officials and guests
that this was a place of gentility
and grace. Suddenly, welling in his breast
a wave of longing for his native place
dimmed his eyes with tears, took his breath away.
He tried to hide all this, shielding his face,
unaware that those he passed along the way
could not see him and so he moved unseen
towards the chamber of the king and queen.

Still screened from sight, he now stood face to face
before the king and queen in the great hall.
He knelt and stretched his hands to embrace
Arete's knees. Athena now let fall
the god mist that had hidden him from view
so far. All were hushed. Was this sorcery?
A stranger in their midst, out of the blue!
Under their eyes, Odysseus made his plea
"Queen Arête. He who is on his knees
before you, is a man whose life is pain;
a man so desperate that he will seize
any chance to see his home again.
May the gods smile on all assembled here
and let me bring my story to your ear."

He went silent then, bowed to the company,
then crossed the room, squatting at the fireside.
Nobody stirred or spoke - eventually
Echeneus broke the silence and replied
"As elder here, I view this stranger's plight
as but a challenge that the gods have thrown
to test our hospitality tonight.
Make a place for this man beside the throne
and when he has had chance to drink and dine,
give this poor man sympathetic hearing."
Alcinous, calm in power, made a sign
and an extra place was set beside the king
with the king's own son vacating his seat.
Alcinous bade Odysseus come and eat.

And so, sitting on his appointed chair,
the lord Odysseus settled down to dine.
Later that night, when all assembled there
had eaten and drained sweet homegrown wine
Alcinous spoke to the company
"My clansmen! Hear me now before you go
your separate ways. I call on this assembly
to grant this guest a festive day - a show
of our sporting and musical renown
and make offerings to the gods on high
so that he can tell the wonders of our town
to his own clansmen, distant though they lie.
Let all depart now, each one taking rest
before we give this send-off to our guest."

And so, the guests departed from the room
leaving Odysseus with the family there.
Recognising the work of her own loom
in his cloak, the queen held him in a stare.
"Stranger. I have three questions for you.
All assembled here tonight heard you claim
you were shipwrecked on your shore. Is that true?
If so, who gave you that cloak? What's your name?"
The great tactician carefully replied
"All this you ask of me I will narrate.
Years ago, my ship was sunk. I should have died
with all my crew but this was not my fate
I clung to a beam; Athena sent to me
and drifted nine days and nights on open sea."

"I was cast ashore, battered by the sea,
on Ogygia, half lifeless on the sand.
This was the nymph Calypso's territory,
a gift from her father Atlas' hand.
Calypso was a goddess with such wiles,
such beauty of form, such enchanting face.
She fed me and nursed me then with tender smiles
and coaxing and voluptuous embrace
promised that I would stay forever young
if I kept her company in bed.
She kept me there for years, although my tongue
gave no consent. The one thought in my head
even as her flesh and mine joined as one
was to return to my wife and son."

"For seven years Calypso kept tight rein
then from the gods on high a stern command.
I was to be freed from that sweet nymph's chain.
She had to yield [a nymph can never stand
against Olympus] and let me sail away
on board a raft I built. She made a breeze
to speed me on my course. Day after day,
seventeen in all, across open seas
I sailed or rowed. But then a sudden blast
heaved up huge waves that blotted out the sky
and split my raft in pieces, deck and mast.
So many times, it seemed that I must die
until by chance or fate I washed up where
a smooth inlet lay not far from here."

"Later on, when I recovered breath,
I moved inland, crawled under olive trees,
and rested soundly there: sleep like death
and slept there until noon next day with leaves
my only covering. I woke to sounds
of maidens playing ball along the beach.
It was your daughter, with her maids and friends.
Dressed just in leaves, I made bold to beseech
your good daughter to help me in my plight
and this she did with royal courtesy
with food and drink to slake my appetite
and these clothes to wear that your majesty
has recognised. And so, my story stands
and I am here; my fate is in your hands."

Alcinous listened to his guest then said
"My child did well in all respects but one
she should have brought you here herself instead
of leaving you seek entry here alone."
To this Odysseus tactfully replied
"Sir. Your good daughter did no wrong at all.
It was my decision that I should bide
my time before I set foot in this hall.
To see her in a strange man's company
might well have made for gossip in the streets."
Alcinous nodded, pleased with this reply
then ordered that the finest rugs and sheets
be used to make a soft bed for his guest,
then left Odysseus to enjoy his rest.

Music, Dancing, Feasting and Sport

Odysseus, raider of great cities, slept
until rose-hued dawn lit the eastern sky
With king Alcinous at his side they stepped
from the court to the place of assembly.
A large crowd gathered, each one summoned there
by Athena, disguised in voice and form
as the royal crier. Most of them came to stare
at this godlike stranger driven here by storm.
Alcinous addressed them then. "Our new friend
nameless to me still, is no stranger to woe
and needs our help to reach his journey's end.
Let two and fifty of our oarsmen go
and rig a ship and moor it in the bay.
When this is done rejoin our games today."

When all was done as Alcinous decreed
each crew man returned to the festive fare
in the banquet hall - a lavish spread indeed!
The minstrel Demodocus was led in there
[the Muse who lent him sweet airs took his sight]
to a studded chair, food placed at his side
and wine as well, his harp strings all tuned tight.
Then, when hunger and thirst were turned aside
the minstrel sang of Troy's siege by the Greeks.
Odysseus placed his cloak across his face
to mask the tears coursing down his cheeks
dried them quickly, so as to leave no trace.
Only the king noticed, sitting at his side
and heard the low groans as Odysseus cried.

To raise the saddened spirit of his guest
Alcinous called all athletes to the track
saying to Odysseus "You will see the best
of runners here today - we have no lack
of boxers, jumpers, discus throwers too."
The games commenced, with racing to the fore
ending with the discus [one of the crew
threw it further than had been done before]
Then Euryalus, who had won the wrestling bout
said to Odysseus "Why don't you compete?
Just looking at you now there is no doubt
you have the making of a fine athlete.
We'll let you enter any sport you choose
unless you are afraid that you will lose?"

Odysseus answered with his usual guile
"I won't compete with young men such as you.
Having come through my own demanding trial
for long long years, my sporting days are through."
Euryalus said "The reason is quite clear
my friend. You haven't any skill at sports
and don't want to reveal this weakness here.
You call to mind skippers you meet at ports
that trudge and traffic goods from town to town,
worn out before their time, inventing tales
of brave exploits at games or high renown
in warfare. These loud windbags never sail
if there's a chance of danger out at sea.
You are that kind of man, it seems to me."

Odysseus eyed him coldly and replied
"That was uncalled for friend, and all nonsense.
All men have certain gifts the gods supplied.
In looks a man might seem a fool but sense
and style in oratory will win the crowd.
Yet another man, beautiful in face
may fail to move assemblies, however loud
he talks, for they will not support his case.
Take yourself now - you have a fine physique
and have proved yourself in these sports, I see.
That's all fine, but your reasoning is so weak
and your public insult has angered me.
I won laurels in contests long ago
To prove it now, I will try a discus throw."

Cloaked as he was, he leapt out on the track
and picked a rounded discus, heavier
than those already used and arched his back
then released the stone, whirling through the air
with such a loud hum as it sped and soared
that those watching at his side ducked in fear
under its rushing noise, and then they roared
to see it land so far away, quite clear
of their own champions' efforts through that day.
Athena, disguised now as a judge declared
"This is by far the best throw here today"
The crowd applauded. Then Odysseus stared
Euryalus with stern gaze and shook his head
"With practice, I'd do much better", he said.

Odysseus turned to the crowd, shouting out
"I have been challenged here and will reply
by taking part in any race or bout
against all comers brave enough to try.
Out of respect to my host as his guest
I will not test myself against his son.
As for combat skills, many will attest
my powers at the bow. Some say that none
but Philoctetes could equal my aim,
and he was lost at Troy's great siege, I know
leaving Heracles, that godlike name
the only one to test me with the bow
I might be beaten in a sprinting race;
Tired by rough seas, my legs have lost their pace."

When Odysseus finished, the king replied
"You've made your point and made it well, my friend,
but let's put all divisive talk aside.
Before your visit here comes to an end
you shall see our dancers. Far from this place
we are renowned as sailors, but on land
our dancers' nimbleness, their speed and grace
is unsurpassed." He stopped and gave command
for all to gather in the dancing hall.
And soon, poised on its floor of polished wood
waiting for the blind harper to call
them into life, a line of dancers stood.
At a sign from their leader, they all bowed
to the king and queen, to the expectant crowd.

When the blind harper's fingers strummed his strings
the dancers moved with beat and stamp of feet
as one, in pairs, in groups, with reels and swings.
Odysseus knew that nothing could compete
with this virtuosity and stood entranced
watching beside the smiling king and queen.
The young men never rested, when they'd danced
one set they never took a rest between
the end of that before they'd start one more.
The crowd urged them on with clapping hands
and rousing cheers and yelled for an encore
when they were done. Yielding to these demands
they went at it one last time and then they bowed
and took their leave of the applauding crowd.

Alcinous called his two sons to attempt
a dance with ball that no one else could do.
The two young men approached and off they went
at dazzling speed. As one prince danced, the other threw
himself and rolled below the other's feet,
or threw the ball above his brother's head
and caught it to the steady, stamping beat
of a ring of boys. Then the young men sped
in and through the ring as the ball was cast
at their flashing figures but not one throw
touched either man as they went dancing past.
At last they came to rest, each one aglow
with the exertion. "Nothing could compare"
said Odysseus, "To what I have seen here"

Alcinous smiled at this and then cried out
"Now that our guest has honoured us with praise
for our sports and dance, let him have no doubt
that our hospitality far outweighs
our reputation in those ancient arts.
Let us bring him parting gifts of gold
and fine clothing too before he departs.
Now as for Euryalus, if truth be told,
he wants to make amends." Without delay
that young man approached, bronze sword in hand
"To undo the hurt I may have caused today
this is my gift to you. You understand
there was no intention to do you harm."
The two men embraced, walked off arm in arm.

Now all assembled for the evening meal
and as Odysseys moved towards his seat
the princess Nausicaa made this appeal.
"Farewell stranger. Our paths may never meet
in this world again once you sail away.
Remember me who helped you in your woe."
Odysseus bowed, "My lady. You will stay
within my heart, no matter where I go."
The meal commenced, the harper was brought to eat
in a place of honour with the family.
Odysseus carved out a portion of the meat
and called the blind man's guide. "The gods decree
that fine poem deserves high praise to be voiced."
Blind Demodocus inwardly rejoiced.

When the meal was over, Odysseus turned
once more to Demodocus. "Let us hear
how Troy's topless towers were felled and burned.
Sing this for me so when I'm far from here
your skill in song and word I can recall."
The minstrel stirred and then began his lay
of the Greek's long siege outside the city wall
and on until their fleet had sailed away,
leaving Odysseus' wooden horse behind.
The Trojans pulled this through the city gate
thinking it a good sign. They were to find
this very act would shortly seal their fate
when Greeks, stowed in that great horse out of sight
climbed out and took Troy from within that night.

The Lotus Eaters and the Cyclops

Listening to his own glory days recalled
Odysseus placed his hands to hide his tears
Alcinous noticed this and he called
"It's time to finish this as it appears
that our song is not pleasing to our guest.
He has tested our hospitality
and I think he'll say that it's passed the test!
I ask him to reveal - if he's free -
his name and place of birth and why he cried
when our minstrel sang of Troy's bloody end
- a sad tale sure enough - so many died.
It seemed to me to touch your heart, my friend
as if it woke a personal loss in you.
A relative? Some much loved friend you knew?"

Odysseus dried his eyes and then replied
"King Alcinous, your minstrel's skills are rare
and for one who has travelled far and wide
I have not heard his equal anywhere.
How will I start this tale? How will I end?
The gods have tried me in a thousand ways.
But first my name - for you have proved a friend
and your good name I will forever praise.
I am called Odysseus, Laertes' son.
Men count me cunning in war and strategy.
Ithaca is my home. Before my race is done
may I return there to my family.
I have been travelling home for many years
and now will bring that journey to your ears."

"Looking back now, our sailing out of Troy
seems a half remembered dream. Who's to know
if I had enraged the gods or do they annoy
men's petty hopes and plans so they can show
that we on earth are puppets in their hands?
We sailed to Ísmaros, a rocky fort
of the Cicones - good sheep raising lands.
The fighting that first day was fierce but short.
We spared no one, took women slaves away.
I urged my men to make their way on board
knowing it would be death to overstay.
But after weeks of sea life, they were bored
and plundered wine vats despite my command
slaughtered sheep, ate fresh mutton on the strand."

Meanwhile, messages were relayed inland
to rally their main army straight away.
At dawn they came as we snored on the strand
and though my men, with lances kept in play,
made a fight of it, we were driven back
to our anchored ships, the surf stained crimson red.
On open sea, we raised a flag of black
on each masthead to mourn our treasured dead;
six loyal comrades lost from our six crews.
I blamed myself, my weak willed captaincy
for losing men I had no right to lose
knowing I could have stopped this tragedy.
Then Zeus sent a storm; a further grief:
each ship became a separate windblown leaf.

Nine days later we managed to make land
where lotus eaters lived, whose only food
was the lotus flower. I gave command
[and made sure my order was understood]
that three shipmates that I took time to choose
would scout the land and check the locals out
and straight away return with any news
without eating there - for a lurking doubt,
a dark premonition about that place
had anchored in my mind. No one can say
if this instinct is gifted or a grace
from the gods to man so there's time to weigh
risks involved against the uncertainty
of reward, or a form of lunacy?

Curiosity had the upper hand
and so, the chosen three made their way
across a golden beach, then moved inland.
Late afternoon of the following day,
when hope of their return seemed a poor chance,
I led a group of ten to find our friends.
We came upon them, each one in a trance
from gorging on the lotus plant which sends
all those who eat it into ecstasy
so strong they never want to leave the place
where this plant grows. We pleaded with the three
but they were wrapped up in the drug's embrace
looking through, beyond us with lifeless stare,
ignoring us as if we weren't there.

Faced with this madness, I had to crack the whip
in case this drugged stupor spread to my crew
[already the news had boarded each ship
with men asking to taste this lotus too]
I ordered our search team to draw their swords
and drive the three to where our ship lay moored.
They wept and screamed but we pushed them towards
the golden beach and got them back on board.
There we tied them to a rowing seat
to keep them safe until their minds were clear,
I warned the rest of them if they should eat
the lotus they would be imprisoned here
and never return home. Without delay
our rowers dipped their oars. We were away!

Soon after this, an island loomed ahead
near to where the Cyclops lived - great brutes.
They had no laws, no tribal rules to shed
light on disagreements; sorting all disputes
through violent means. They lived apart
in caves, each man mistreating wife or child.
They neither plough nor sow, nor have the art
of cultivating vines though these grow wild
around them everywhere. Wild mountain goats
roam unploughed fiends and unplanted hilly ground.
We made safe harbour there, our anchored boats
hidden in a deep fog that muffled sound,
so that we landed undetected there,
gliding towards the shore through the thick white air.

As the pale rose light of dawn lit the sky,
we woke refreshed and proceeded to explore.
The island teemed with goats, not one being shy
of our approach [never having before
being hunted by any man]. Without sweat
we killed nine for each ship, ten for mine;
set up campfire and feasted on fresh meat,
then sampled from our plunder store of wine.
Looming darkly ahead, before our eyes
the Cyclops mainland neared. It was so near
we could see smoke from their campfires rise
into the clear sky across the bay, could hear
the bleating of their flocks. We slept that night
on the curving shore under clear moonlight.

Next morning, as rose hued dawn lit the sky
I gathered all hands from our twelve ship fleet
"Old shipmates. Hear me out! My crew and I
will row out to the mainland. We may meet
with savage or civil men in that place
[gods alone hold the future in their hands]
but we'll deal with what greets us face to face".
I gave the nod. We hauled out of the sand
and dipped our oars in line and eased away,
stroking across the smooth glass of the sea
towards that dark land mass, brooding on the bay.
Watching my oarsmen's practiced fluency,
I smiled with pride, and yet a sense of dread
pressed on my heart, wondering what lay ahead.

It took no time to row across the bay,
to beach the ship and hide it in a cove.
We walked the shoreline then and made our way
to where, perched on a hill, a yawning cave
gaped above a slanting strip of beach.
Beside it we saw sheep, penned in a fold
fashioned from slabs of stone, made fast by beech
and oak tree stumps. And then our blood ran cold
to see a giant, emerge from that cave mouth.
The size of him! His footsteps shook the ground.
We could have turned away, got safely out
but something did not let me turn around.
Instead, I chose twelve men, my very best
and left the ship there, guarded by the rest.

I knew there could be danger in our plan,
and brought a jar of brandy that packed some punch,
sensing that this part monster, part man
might be pleased with such a gift [just a hunch].
A priest had given me this potent stuff
at Ismaros when I spared his life there.
He warned me that one mouthful was enough
to floor a man and he himself took care
to mix one cupful of this heady drink
in twenty cups of water and yet the taste
stayed strong and pure, leaving him on the brink
of stupor. I slung the jar to my waist
and then our group climbed briskly to the place,
wondering what adventures we were to face.

The giant was not at home when we got there,
out herding his fat sheep until sunfall.
So, at our ease, we looked around his lair
drying racks that sagged with cheese lined one wall,
while milking pails and vessels brimmed with whey
stood on the cavern floor. We came outside
the cave, blinking under the light of day
and found a field behind, fenced on each side
by wooden pens, constructed carefully.
There lambs and kids, arranged by size and age,
were safely housed. My men came out to me
"Let's take these animals, empty every cage
down to our ship, then take the cheeses too."
That was the advice I got from my crew.

I should have listened to my men that day;
sound advice should not be cast aside
but I was curious [that is my way]
to meet the caveman. So, we stayed inside,
sampling his range of cheeses on bread.
At last, we heard him coming and the place
trembled with the sound. We crouched in dread
of that huge and hairy figure, that face
with one glittering eye. A load of wood
he'd carried inside was dumped on the floor;
the hollow cave reverberated with the thud.
To our horror then, he made a makeshift door;
a massive granite slab he dragged to block
the entrance with this solid wall of rock.

He took a wooden stool and without delay
milked his bleating ewes that he'd brought in
before he'd sealed the cave from light of day.
He whisked the milk then, thickening its skin,
sieved out the curds, letting the whey stand
in bowls. He'd take this later with his food.
When this was done, he knelt and poked and fanned
ash covered sparks into flame. Then he stood
and in the sudden leaping glare of light
that searched out every corner of that place
he saw us, huddled, shivering with fright.
He stood stock still. We saw his massive face
loom over us, that eye a glaring ball.
We retreated, our backs against the wall.

"Strangers" he roared. "Who are you? From what place
have you travelled and why have you come here?
Are you pirates who cast men's lives like dice
in search of plunder? Answer! Let me hear!"
His booming voice, like thunder in our ears
set our hearts racing in our chests with dread.
But all the same, I somehow hid my fears,
stood before the surly giant and said
"We are Achaeans, blown off course by gales
on our return from Troy which we destroyed
after a long and savage siege. Our sails
have brought us here. Great Zeus would be annoyed
if sea travellers are not shown courtesy.
That is our right - the custom of the sea."

The great brute glared, rage pulsing on his face
"We Cyclopes are not bound by your sea rules!
Your puny gods hold no sway in this place,
their wills may bind timid small-minded fools
like you but we are unafraid and free.
But now, my little man, I'd like to know
are there more of you than this company?
Where is your ship at anchor?" I'm not slow
and discerned his real intent straight away.
"Our ship broke up on rocks at your land's end.
Our other shipmates drowned - we've made our way
to your home today hoping you can send
us homeward on the last leg of our trip,
help us with wood and tools to build a ship."

What happened next, such horror to recall;
the brute reached down and snatched two of my crew
then smashed their heads to pieces off the wall,
dismembered them, started to crunch, and chew
his way through innards, flesh, and marrow bones.
Appalled we cried out, powerless to intervene
but Cyclops, heedless of our groans
continued feasting. The sight was obscene.
He finished with gulping draughts of whey
then slumped into sleep. I drew my blade
to pierce his liver through but pulled away,
knowing if I killed this monster we stayed
entombed with him, sealed in from the light.
I'd have to make a new plan overnight.

Next morning the Cyclops, refreshed from sleep,
built a fire and then, as he'd done before,
took out a wooden stool to milk his sheep.
When this was done, he snatched up from the floor
two more of our dear friends and had his snack.
Then he moved the massive door to make way
for his sheep to move out, then pushed it back,
trapping us inside. He moved away
whistling to his flock. Soon all was quiet.
I stood beside the fire, addressed my crew
told them my plan I had hatched overnight
to escape from here, avenge our comrades too.
It was a risky scheme I had conceived,
but it was worth the risk we all believed.

A massive wooden pole stood by the wall,
used by the Cyclops as a staff or club.
I chopped out a section, six foot tall
and dragged it to my men, told them to rub
and scrape it smooth and point it like a spear.
We toughened it on the fire, turned round
from time to time as you'd turn meat, for fear
it might burn. This done, we hid it on the ground
under a steaming heap of sheep manure.
Then we tossed for it in order to see
who might join me [I wanted to be sure
I had the bravest of the company]
but four men I'd have chosen anyway
won the toss. Fate or chance? It's hard to say

At sunset, the huge shepherd and his flock
returned. Both rams and ewes were brought inside
before Cyclops replaced the slab of rock
in its place. Then, leaving the rams aside,
he sat down to milk the ewes as before.
When this was done, he lifted two more men
and ate them there - a horror scene of gore!
Knowing I had to act right there and then
I approached the beast, holding out to him
a bowl of that strong drink. "Try this for taste"
I said "You see I've filled it to the brim
to suit your appetite. It'll go to waste
if you don't drink it, it's too strong for us.
We'd meant it as an offering to Zeus."

He grabbed the bowl and gulped the heady brew,
then licked his lips and belched contentedly
"Give me another bowl and while you do
tell me your name. You'll get a gift from me."
He drank three bowls. I watched the drink take hold
as the Cyclops stumbled, his face a flushed red
"You asked me my name - let it be told.
I'm Nohbdy." "Well, Nohbdy" he said
"As my reward to you for your fine drink
I'll keep you to the end - the last to die
when I've eaten all your friends." I watched him sink
into a drunken sleep which closed his eye.
Droplets of liquor and hits of blood gore
dribbled from his mouth. He started to snore.

I knew this was our opportunity
and so, we dragged the stake we had prepared.
We placed it on the fire carefully,
charring its arrowed tip until it flared,
as if to burn, then pulled it out once more.
Now five of us hoisted it chest high
and ran it across the cavern floor
and rammed it deep into the Cyclops' eye.
I leaned on it, to make it grind and twist
as a shipwright, making planks, turns a drill.
Scorched blood and body tissue steamed and hissed
around that molten spike. We held it till
we heard the eye roots snap, the eyeball boil;
We stood back then, exhausted from our toil.

The Cyclops bellowed, screams of agony
echoed in that sealed off cave, a storm of sound.
We fell back in fear then weak at the knee
as the great blind searching hands reached and found
the bloody spike and pulled it from the eye
then flung it with a clatter off a wall.
He roared out to his neighbours living by
who clumped outside in answer to his call
"Polyphemus, why don't you let us sleep?
Has some stranger driven your flock away?"
He replied "It's nothing to do with sheep!
Nohbdy's ruined me." "Oh, if that's the way
stop that awful noise and give us rest"
they said, they left. My plan had passed first test.

The Cyclops, half maddened and fully blind
fumbled to wrench the great door stone aside,
then squatted in the breach, hoping to find
with his outstretched hands any fool who tried
to get past him there - no one could escape.
I ran through every strategy and trick
and after time a cunning plan took shape.
The Cyclops' rams were fat, their fleeces thick,
so, using strips of clothing that we found
I tied the rams together, three abreast,
then slung one man in place, securely bound,
under the middle ram. I took the best,
the wooliest for myself and clung there tight.
This done, we waited for the morning light.

When morning came the sheep began to bleat,
restless to head to pasturelands outside.
Still racked with pain, Cyclops, on a seat
checked each ram by patting its back and side
before he let it pass but never felt
underneath the animals as they passed.
Last of all my ram. Now Cyclops knelt
and patted him then asked "Why are you last
today when each other time you are the first?
Are you grieving for my eye? If you could show
me where Nohbdy is hiding I'd burst
his brains across this floor but I well know
you can't do this one thing for me, alas."
He stood up then and let the big ram pass.

Relieved to breathe in open air again
I dropped from my woolly friend and rolled clear
then went back and forth to untie my men.
Quickly we rounded up the flock - the fear
that Cyclops might hear us left us quiet.
We drove them to our waiting ship - the crew
raced up to meet our group but their delight
turned into grief when they knew what we knew.
I had to hush their cries; speed was the key.
We had to board the flock and head out straight
from the rocky inlet to open sea
Anxious to escape our dear comrades' fate
each crewman concentrated on his oar:
We pulled away from that accursed shore.

When we were far from shore, yet in earshot
for shouted words to carry back to land.
I stood astern with anger burning hot
then shouted shorewards through my two cupped hands
"Cruel cannibal who feasted on my crew
how do you like the taste of punishment?"
He heard my words and bent down then threw
a massive boulder in our path. He meant
to sink us but it landed far ahead
of our prow, setting up a massive surge
that pushed our ship backwards. I kept my head,
stopped us with a boat hook, then turned to urge
my men to row 'till we had pulled away
twice as far, safely out of danger's way.

Now further out, I cupped my hands once more
but my crew protested "Leave him alone
or he'll adjust his next throw from the shore
and smash our timbers with a second stone."
I wouldn't heed them, and turned to shout
driven by a sudden need to tell
"If you are asked who burned your eyeball out,
listen to me and mind you listen well.
Know it was Odysseus, Laertes' son,
great warrior and cunning strategist
in revenge for the horror, you have done
to his helpless comrades." I shook my fist
as if to strike the monster with a blow.
"Odysseus from Ithaca, now you know."

The blinded Cyclops answered in dismay
"Odysseus! The very name is doom to me
Telem, who lived here years before this day
was well known for his skill in prophecy.
Among the future things that he foretold
was the loss of my great and only eye
at Odysseus' hand. A giant, brave and bold
I thought might in the future come to try
to carry out that dark and dangerous deed,
using heroic strength - not sly deceit.
Yet here you came, as puny as a weed
and drugged me with your wine and took my sight.
But hear me out, I'll make a deal with you
that might speed you home, get my sight back too."

"Return to me" he said "and I'll appeal
to my father Poseidon to speed your way
to your home. If I do that he might heal
this blackness and let me see the light of day
burnt out by your hand." Now I made reply
"You ate my friends. Do not seek help from me."
With that he prayed, blind eye turned to the sky
"Great father! May bloodshed and savagery
mark this man's home return and lose his friends
and all his fleet of ships, forcing him to sail
with strangers when that lengthy journey ends."
He threw a mighty rock, to no avail
as it fell short, pushing us from shore.
We moved from the island with urgent oar.

We rowed away, without any more ado
to where our fleet lay waiting on our return
and shared the Cyclops' flock among each crew.
I killed the ram I'd clung to, hoping to earn
respite from great Zeus with this sacrifice.
So, we made solemn offerings and took our fill
of dark sweet wine and mutton dipped in spice
until, at dusk, the air turned dark and chill.
I took my rest, tired out by this long day
and slept until the dawn. I roused my men.
We manned the ships, cast mooring ropes away,
then dipped our oars, pulling out again
on the glassy sea. Later we would find
that Zeus was still unmoved, had not changed his mind.

Circe and her dark arts

We rowed right through the day, our grief still raw,
mourning the loss of friends snatched suddenly
and savagely from this world. Then we saw
cliffs ahead - a land floating on the sea
with rampart walls above - a fine stronghold.
Aeolus, the wind king, was ruler here.
Six daughters and six sons made up his household.
He matched them up in twos, six marriage pairs.
We were made welcome at the royal court
with feasts and sport and song by day and night.
Aeolus was all ears to my report
of the Trojan war and took great delight
hearing our adventures since great Troy fell
in talks with me and with my crew as well.

For thirty days we lived in luxury
then Aeolus provisioned us to sail,
and as we left, the lord of winds and sea
gave me a leather bag, sewn neck to tail
containing all the storms that seamen dread.
He hid this bag on deck, wedged at the mast
then twisted silver wire around its head
so not one breath of wind would rise up past
this tightened seal, the danger locked secure.
To speed our progress on our homeward way
when he filled the bag, Aeolus had made sure
to loose the west wind. We made no delay
in raising sails and leaving shore behind
with Ithaca the one thought on my mind.

Nine days and nights we sailed without event
and on the tenth sighted our own dear shore.
By this time, all my energy was spent
for lack of sleep had tired me to the core.
So, I fell asleep then as if one dead
and while I slept, my comrades gathered round
"There's gold and silver in that bag" they said
"All for the captain. Let's share it around,
why should we not profit from this long trip?"
They took the bag from underneath the mast
then untied the wires' tightly knotted grip.
To their horror, they heard a deafening blast
burst from the opened bag, a hurricane!
Our ship pitched back, pushed far from land again.

Was it luck or destiny on our side
that saw us through the worst storms we had seen.
To our surprise, we found ourselves outside
those same high cliffs and ramparts that had been
our point of departure so recently.
With two men at my side, I called once more
to Aeolus, dining with his family.
They rose in shock when we walked in the door,
"Why have you returned? Did we not launch you
on your trip home?" I told my story plain
of my sleep and my avaricious crew,
then asked Aeolus for his help again.
"It's wrong to give help", was his snarled reply
"To any man cursed by the gods on high."

We were driven from that place despite our pleas
then travelled east for six long days and nights,
tired, hard rowing without a helping breeze
until we saw the Laestrygorvian heights
ahead of us and anchored in a cove,
ringed by walls of stone on either side.
These cliffs converged as if to touch above
our berthed fleet. My own black ship I tied
to a jutting rock in a nearby bay.
As we marched back to where the others were,
we noticed a strange stillness in the day;
no call of bird or animal, no stir
of leaf on tree, the sea unrippled glass;
they only sound our footsteps on the grass.

We joined the rest. I picked three men to scout
this new land and report back all they found.
Inland they met a girl who pointed out
the local king's [her father] large compound.
His name was Antiphates, a savage giant
who came out snarling when our men came by.
He seized one man and tore him joint to joint,
gobbled his flesh and sucked his marrow dry.
The other two in terror raced away
but he raised up the whole tribe in their wake;
enormous on the skyline, scenting prey.
Try as they might, my two men couldn't shake
those hunters off their tracks although they tried
every trick they knew to lose them or to hide.

Back to our anchored fleet they chased the pair
and then hailed massive boulders from on high
on the tethered ships. Death dropped from the air
as decks were smashed. I watched my shipmates die
on their boats. If they jumped overboard,
they were stabbed like fish with sword blade or spear
and hauled away. I ran and drew my sword
and sliced my own ship's rope to move us clear
from our rocky anchorage and with my crew
leapt aboard, each man desperate at his oar,
rowing in mortal dread for we well knew
we had to move out far enough from the shore
to be out of range on the open sea,
safely delivered from that butchery.

We spurted out of range, each stroke of oar
powered by fear, and soon reached open sea.
Then we recovered breath. Our hearts were sore
remembering comrades lost so brutally.
Our next port of call was the island base
of Circe, daughter of Helios, god of sun.
With land in sight, we found a mooring place,
anchored and tied up. When this was done,
I climbed to higher ground above the bay
while my comrades slept, to explore the land
and saw a curling smoke wisp, reddish grey,
rising from a residence tall and grand.
To me it seemed the dwelling of a queen;
I moved to tell my crew what I had seen.

As I retraced my steps along the way
back to the ship, I chanced upon a deer,
a massive stag. He wheeled to move away
but was too slow by far. I flung my spear
and hit him in the spine. He tried to move
but toppled twitching and then lay still.
I braced myself against his dead weight to remove
my weapon from his back then dragged my kill
downhill to the ship. That mighty weight
was too much for me to bear alone.
And so that night we drank strong wine and ate
our fill of venison. For those friends gone
from us we raised a toast in memory
of our shared adventures by land and sea.

When morning came, I stood the men in line
and set out two platoons, twenty two in each.
Eurylochus led one, the other group was mine.
One group would stay behind, patrol the beach
and guard our ship - our one way out of here;
the other explore the countryside.
Lots were drawn to ensure that all was fair
from a soldier's cap fashioned from dog hide.
Eurylochus' lot was first to come out
and so, with half of our remaining crew
he marched away across the hills to scout
Circe's island home. Not one among us knew
as we watched them climbing upwards from the shore,
the hellish sorcery they had in store.

Our comrades marched away as we remained
beside the ship. They soon found Circe's hall
outside of which mountain lions, yellow-maned,
and wolves lay resting, mild in their soft spell.
With tails wagging, they rose and then drew near
Eurylochus' men, like household hounds who spy
their master at the door and show no fear.
Our friends met their yellow eyes and passed by,
unnerved by the strangeness of the scene.
Inside they could see weaving at a loom
bright ambrosial fabric, Circe the queen.
She was singing. Her voice caressed the room,
beguiling, magical and honey sweet.
They stood entranced, powerless to move their feet.

Sensing their presence, she moved from her loom
and welcomed them, leading them inside
to where places were set in a dining room.
Eurylochus alone remained outside
sensing danger. Meanwhile Circe served wine,
adding a secret potion to each glass.
They drank her toast, and all were turned to swine
the instant they let the addled liquid pass
their lips - each one a rooting, grunting pig!
She penned them in a sty and shut the gate,
all squealing at high pitch. She watched them dig
for acorns in the earth. Each knew his fate
since each one's mind was untouched by her spell:
Such knowledge adding horror to their hell.

Eurylochus, shocked by what had taken place,
went running towards the shore to tell the crew.
In their presence, tears streaming from his face,
he could not speak at first, but then all knew
what horrors had been cast by Circe's spell.
I heard his grim report and then I roared
"Retrace your steps with me and I will kill
this evil witch with one stroke of my sword."
Eurylochus pleaded "Such bravery
is mad. Our friends will not return again.
We must save ourselves, escape by sea.
Circe is a goddess, cannot be slain
by mortal blade or trickery of mind.
We must go now and leave the rest behind."

The crew pressed round and each one had his say
all voting to leave this place by next tide.
I would not change my mind, retraced the way,
taken by Eurylochus, I walked inside
a hushed and shady grove. A figure stood
as if it had been waiting for me there
and moved to stop me going through the wood
with a golden wand upraised. I could swear
it was the great god Hermes in disguise
as a young man. He took my hand and said
"If you try to free your friends from the ties
that turned them into swine, you'll never tread
the halls of far-off Ithaca again.
I can help. Hear me and I will explain."

"There is one sacred plant that will negate
the curse that Circe placed upon your crew.
This holy herb will keep your thinking straight
if she should come with wand in hand at you.
Unsheathe your sword and let her see your blade
and she will bend to you and yield her bed;
a comfort you must take so you can trade
that pleasure for her promise that she shed
the spell that she has cast. Get her to vow
that she will keep her word and let you free
or you will become as your friends are now,
wrapped in swinish form. Behind this tree
nestling in its shades is where this plant thrives.
It will save you and save your comrades' lives."

The glittering god searched in among the trees,
tugged a blackrooted plant with milk white flower
out of the resisting earth with deft ease.
It's said that gods alone can wield the power
for this plant will not yield to mortal hand.
So, I took the molú and made my way
to Circe's mansion, on through meadowland
and yet another wood. Without delay
I left this second forest in my wake
and found myself at last standing alone
at Circe's porch. There was so much at stake
that for a while I paused, chilled to the bone
despite the fierce sun burning overhead;
my heart a pounding urgent drum of dread.

As if she'd heard the beating of my heart,
out of nowhere Circe stood at my side
and softly welcomed me. I played my part,
striding past a hallway long and wide
to her dining room. There she led the way
to a silver studded throne and placed my feet
on a low stool. She then produced a tray
holding a bowl of tampered wine, honey sweet.
Protected by the plant, whose milky flower
I'd chewed on as I'd travelled to this place
I knew her potion had no magic power.
She came forward, a cruel look on her face,
and with wand upraised whispered in my ear
"Down to the sty, join my other pigs there."

I heard her out then made my own reply,
drawing my sword, pressing its whetted blade
against her throat. With an astonished cry
she slid downwards, as if to faint, then laid
her hands upon my knees. "My secret brew
is one whose spell no mortal can withstand.
That prophecy of Hermes must be true,
that great Odysseus would one day stand
alone before me and unlock my heart.
Sheathe your weapon and come with me to bed;
we two will mingle there in love's soft art."
She rose and gently touched my face and said
"Oh, son of Laertes! Let us not delay
what we both desire. I will lead the way."

To this I replied "Listen to me well.
Do you think me soft, so easily swayed
by these seductive skills? You've used a spell
to bewitch half my crew and would have played
the same trick on myself. I have a fear
if I am stripped and sated by your side,
that you will try again: a price too dear
for me to pay - joining my men outside,
a grunting, rooting prisoner in a sty.
But if I agree to join you in your bed
you must first swear an oath to Zeus on high
you'll bring no more enchantment on my head."
I finished speaking then and let her stand,
watched her like a hawk, sword in my hand.

She kissed my hand and rose without delay
and swore, as I had asked, to Zeus on high
that I would be unharmed, then led the way
to her soft pillowed bed, sweet hours went by
in mingled pleasuring, in ecstasy
so intense at times I thought my heart would burst.
We revelled there in carnal harmony
all day 'till pangs of hunger and of thirst
reined us in as the sunset sank down west.
One of Circe's nymphs - she had four in all,
filled a bubbling bathtub to my waist
and bathed me and smoothed me with oil,
massaged me head to toe with heated stones,
easing the soreness of my joints and bones.

When I was dried and dressed, she led the way
to where Circe would sit with me to eat.
The other nymphs had laboured through the day
setting tableware, placing stools for feet
with candles lit and incense in the air.
Circe embraced me and we sat to dine
and everything was sheer perfection there;
each plate a wonder, such exquisite wine.
Though I needed to sate my appetite,
my mind was elsewhere, giving me no joy;
Thinking of my comrades' inhumane plight;
my brave shipmates who'd sailed with me from Troy.
And so, I sat and brooded in dismay:
when wine was served, I moved my glass away.

As I sat there and never touched a crust
Circe questioned me "Is something amiss
with this food or drink? Is it you don't trust
the oath I made then sealed it with a kiss?"
I met her lovely eyes with mine and cried
"What captain in my place would drink or eat
if his crew were not dining by his side?"
Circe nodded and quickly left her seat,
long staff in her hand, unlocked the sty.
She drove the pigs indoors, then stroked each one
with her wand. In the blinking of an eye
they were men again and the spell undone.
We hugged each other, shouted, laughed and cried
and Circe stood there smiling at my side side.

When I'd embraced those men, I'd thought I'd lost,
Circe commanded me to bring the crew
guarding our ship to a reunion feast.
I hurried there without more ado.
When they saw me, they raced in sheer delight
to crowd around me, loud shouts and happy tears
You've seen in farmyards, it's a common sight
when cows return to pasture, it appears
as if the calves go giddy in their joy
all stampeding towards their mothers' sides.
So too my friends who fought with me at Troy
who crewed with me through overwhelming tides
as well as countless dangers on dry land,
thronged round me, taking turns to shake my hand.

I addressed my comrades when they fell quiet
"All who marched inland are safe and well.
We are to join them, in a feast tonight;
welcome guests in Circe's enchanted hall."
They obeyed me as they had always done
and turned to go but Eurylochus stayed
"Are you all madmen" he cried "everyone
who visits her is unmanned, then remade
as a pig or wolf or lion or other beast.
Good friends of ours were lost in Cyclops' cave
because of what Odysseus asked. I ceased
to trust him when he sent dear friends, so brave
yet so helpless as lambs before the butcher's knife.
Stay away from Circe's house. Save your life!"

Though he was my kinsman, I had in mind
to draw the blade that swung against my side
and slice his throat but the others lined
between us there and turned my rage aside.
"Odysseus" they cried "leave him waiting here
while we follow you." We marched away.
Eurylochus followed us out of fear
that my anger might return should he stay.
Meanwhile the other group, at Circe's command
were bathed, dressed and sitting down to eat
when we arrived. To see my valiant band
reunited was a joy so strong and sweet.
At first, I was stunned, unable to speak
then greeted them, tears coursing down my cheek.

Then spoke Circe, loveliest of all the gods
"Heed this Odysseus, master mariner.
All know how you have fought against steep odds
on land and sea; your fame has travelled far.
It is high time for you to sit and rest.
Enjoy fine wine and food then anchor here
each member of your crew will be my guest."
We all agreed and stayed on for a year
until one blazing summer afternoon
my friends approached. "Captain! Shake off this trance.
We need to sail for home and sail there soon."
I saw the sense in this and at first chance
asked Circe to honour her promise made
and let us sail home, for we had overstayed.

And so, as daylight ebbed, I spoke my mind
to Circe as we lingered in her bed
"My friends press me that we will never find
our way back home to Ithaca" I said.
"They gave me no peace on this, by night or day
those times when you are not around to hear."
She replied "You will not be forced to stay
but you will never reach your home from here
unless you go where mortals dread to go
to Hades' underworld, that fearsome place.
Blind Tiresias will meet you there and show
you trials and challenges that you will face
when you land on Ithaca's stony shore;
only he can tell you what lies in store."

On hearing this I felt a dread so chill
that I shook and shivered in her warm bed.
When I had tossed and turned and had my fill
of dark despair, I turned to her and said
"Who will be my pilot, my trusted guide?
No man has ever journeyed to that place
and mingled with the shades of those that died?"
Circe turned around and stroked my face
"When you leave here, sail out to open sea,
move with the northern wind and hold that tack
until you reach the ocean's end. You'll see
Persephone's grove fringed with trees still and black
and birdless there, steer past the rip tide's roar
and her house of death will show its door."

"When you set foot on that desolate strand
do this: Dig a well shaft one forearm square
and pour in milk and honey with one hand.
With the other spill wine and water there
for the numberless dead as an offering.
Pledge then to those faint shades should you return
to Ithaca in safety that you'll bring
a choice heifer from your herd which you will burn
as sacrifice. Vow too that you will kill
a jet black lamb, the best one on your farm
for blind Teiresias. That blood you'll spill
first to honour him then to ward off harm
from the restless phantoms that you will find
when you leave the living world behind."

"Now hear me out! The next thing you must do
when you land on that bleak, deserted strand
is to sacrifice a lamb and an ewe,
facing the gloom of Erebos. Then stand
and you will see the faint host of the dead
emerge, like driven leaves into the air.
Stand your ground then and keep a level head.
Draw sword from hip, crouch down when they draw near,
ward off those surging phantoms with your blade
until you see the one you want to see,
Tieresias, alone of all the shades
charged forever with the gift of prophecy.
Listen to what this sightless shade will say,
he'll lead you safely home - he'll show the way."

Next morning, I assembled all the crew
"The lady Circe says we may depart"
Without a word they all moved, as men do
who hear a spoken message with their heart.
But even from this place I did not go
without a soldier lost under my care.
His name was Elpênor, a little slow,
no great shakes in combat, the youngest there.
To taste last night's cool air, he'd made his way
on to Circe's roof, then fell asleep with wine.
Our downstairs voices woke him the next day.
By accident or by a god's design,
he lost his balance, falling to the ground
and snapped his neck. We never heard a sound.

This young man died without being given due
burial rites. Meanwhile, down at the shore
I stood and addressed my assembled crew
and told them of the trial they had in store.
When they heard all this, they were stunned and still,
then questioned me with bitter words and shouts.
I let them grumble, let their worries spill,
then picked my time to ease their fears and doubts.
"We must take this course, it's the only way
we can return to those we love." At last
they went along with me. We sailed away
from Circe's harbour. Tethered to the mast
we found a ram and ewe she had left there.
She had been on board, none of us aware.

In the Land of the Dead

Out of nowhere, or stirred at Circe's request,
a canvas-bulging breeze sped us from shore.
All day we sailed and when the sun dipped west,
we found ourselves where no man had gone before.
A land where winter reigns throughout the year,
a cheerless place, wrapped up in cloud and snow,
no sunlit warmth. This land was harsh and drear.
We loosed, then led ashore the ram and ewe,
then dug a votive pit one forearm square.
I poured in milk and honey, then sweet wine
and water, then addressed the dead in prayer,
vowing to kill as a thanksgiving sign
the choice heifer from my own pastureland
back home if we returned there safe and sound.

To Tierêsias, I'd swore I'd sacrifice
a jet black lamb should he guide our way
back to Ithaca with his keen advice.
Those pledges done, I made no more delay
but cut the throat of ram and ewe and spilled
their still warm blood into the votive pit.
Now the dead thronged round and the air was filled
with rustling shapes and cries, like bats that flit
in swarms out of the mouth of caves at dark.
Brides and mature wives, old men in pain,
parents, children and soldiers with the mark
of their last combat on their skin, those slain
in violent argument by friend or foe.
They moved around us, emerging from below.

They came with groans and cries from every side,
trembling the air around our fearful heads.
Remembering the words of Circe, our guide,
we offered our sacrifices to the dead.
That done, we kept the surging ghosts at bay
as they massed around the pit like moths to a flame,
using our drawn swords. Once we cleared the way
with one grey group we had to do the same
with the next swarm of restless, twisting ghosts.
We wondered when Tierêsias would appear
to make his presence felt among the hosts.
It was to meet his shade that we were here,
this blind seer was the one who's prophecy
would guide our homecoming. He held the key.

A young man's shade veered towards us suddenly
more vivid than the other phantoms there.
It was Elpênor, of our company
who had died with not one of us aware.
He'd been left unburied, a lonely end
as we marched from Circe's hall to our ship.
Now I wept in pity for my young friend
and asked "Before we started on this trip
you were in Circe's hall; now you are here?"
"Captain, I slept on Circe's roof last night.
Next day, still tired by wine, with head unclear,
I missed a ladder rung and fell from height
snapping my neck bone, and my spirit fled
to this dark place, this kingdom of the dead."

He went on, "There is one thing to be done
I want you to promise me on the head
of your own wife, your father and your son
after leaving this grim world of the dead
you will build a cairn for me if you land
on Ithaca and plant on it the oar
I used at sea, under your command.
Do this for me when you tie up on that shore
to appease the gods on high. Let me hear
your word on this for this unhappy shade
will be doomed to wander in worry here
until those funeral honours have been paid."
I pledged to do this task with all my heart
and stood in sorrow, watching him depart.

Then I saw, among all the grey ghosts there
my own mother. I hadn't seen her face
since I'd first sailed to Troy. Now she was here!
I ached to speak with her and to embrace
her tenderly but she just turned aside.
Tieresias came next, tapping out his way
with a golden staff and stood by my side.
"Odysseus! Why have you left the light of day,
the world of busy men under the sun
for this cold, joyless region of the dead?
Put down your sword. Only when that is done
may I taste the votive blood you have shed
allowing me to voice a prophecy
and guide your homeward way across the sea."

I stepped aside and sheathed my bright sword
to let him taste the blood of lamb and ewe,
then stayed there quiet to hear his every word,
knowing his gift of prophecy would show
my proper homeward course and chart it well.
At last, he spoke "Great captain! A fair wind
is all you need, but this I can foretell.
In revenge for his son whom you left blind,
Poseidon will put dangers in your way
by every means he has at his command.
So, listen carefully to what I say:
my inner vision tells me you will land
on Ithaca with crew or else alone
depending on a test that must be done."

Tieresias continued and now his voice
soared upwards on the wings of prophecy.
"How you get home is dependent on a choice
you will make. Your journey across the sea
will bring you to Thrinakia's green land
where fat herds of Helios roam at will.
Ensure that you, and those that you command
do not harm these cattle; for if you spill
their blood with spear or sword you'll arrive
in Ithaca alone, without your crew,
the sole survivor to reach home alive.
If cows are killed, this also will come true:
strangers will bring you home. There you will face
dangers in your own house you must erase."

"When you disembark at journey's end
you will find your household in disarray.
Your wife deserted there, without one friend
to give her sound advice - she has no say
in her own house. A loud and dog rough crew
camp in her dining hall against her will,
carousing day and night. These ruffians queue
to court your wife and will continue till
she gives in at last, certain that you're dead.
You'll make them pay in blood for what they've done
through open force, or else by stealth instead
and kill the lot. You will not be alone
when battle rages; your son and heir
will be at your shoulder as you fight there."

"When you have cleared that nest of vipers out
you then must make a journey to atone
for all that bloody work - for have no doubt
the deeds of every mortal are well known
among the gods on high. Walk overland,
shouldering your smooth bladed, trusted oar.
Keep walking until one day you will stand
among those who never heard the ocean's roar
or tasted salt on meat or seen a ship.
"Is that a spade you carry?" one will say.
Once you hear this, straightaway plant its tip
in yielding soil and later that same day
make sacrifice to every god in turn,
then leave the oar behind you and return."

"On returning home, you must do the same
atonement rites but this time by the sea,
praying to all the gods, each one by name.
If you do this, Olympus will decree
that you will have a fine life, rich in years
and die a soft death sleeping in your bed."
He was silent. I begged him through my tears
"Before I leave this kingdom of the dead
tell me why my mother ignores her son.
How may we speak?" Tieresias replied
"For this to happen, first this must be done:
Lead her to the pit dug at your side
and let her sip the blood. Do that much;
but take heed; you may only talk not touch."

He turned away, his prophecy complete
and I moved swiftly to my mother's shade,
let her sip the blood, then sat at her feet.
"My child! Why are you here? Why have you strayed
into this dreary kingdom of the dead?
Did you return from that long Trojan war
back to your waiting wife and son?" she said
"Or do you journey still, travelling far
from your beloved home by land and sea?"
"I've come to the land of the death" I replied
"To seek direction home through prophecy.
In our travels, so many men have died
my once proud fleet is now one single ship
through twists of fate or my poor leadership."

"Dear mother, tell me what has brought you here,
long illness, sudden end or accident?
My wife Penelope, I long to hear
how she is faring, how her days are spent,
on long lonely nights does she sleep alone?
And Telemachus, surely a young man now.
I left him newborn, this son I've never known.
There is one final thing I need to know,
how does my father bear his double pain,
his son and wife both gone, one lost one dead?
How I hunger to see these three again
to touch their faces, to taste wine and bread
in Ithaca with all my travelling done.
Tell me news of my father, wife and son."

Sensing my thirst for news, she made reply
"No other man takes up your cherished place
in your wife's heart, her lonely nights go by
warmed by hope that she will see your face
though suitors press on her, she never yields.
Telemachus applies his energy
as magistrate and runs the house and fields.
Your father shuns all joy, all company,
sleeps among his slaves in a lowly bed,
pining for your return. That selfsame ache
has brought me to this outpost of the dead,
to this sad sleep from which I cannot wake.
You were your parents only pride and joy.
How I curse the day you sailed to Troy!"

I saw deep anguish shadowed in her face
as she finished speaking. She turned to me
but when I reached out, desperate to embrace,
she went sifting through my hands like mercury.
"What heartless punishment is this" I cried
to be so far apart and yet so near?
"We are not flesh and bone here" she replied,
"all is burned to ash in the funeral bier
insubstantial as dreams or wisps of cloud.
"You must depart this place, for all men know
the living and the dead are not allowed
remain together. But before you go
remember all of this so you may tell
these marvels to your wife. Note them well."

My mother left, then other shades appeared
in groups, eager to sip the votive blood
that they might talk to me. As each group neared
I drew my sword, ensuring each one stood
in line so that we could meet privately.
First one I met was Tyro. One hot day
she bathed naked, thinking none could see
in a rippling stream pool. But as she lay
disguised in that whirlpool, all foam and flow
Poseidon surged within her - divine bliss,
and whispered his name to her, and let her know
she would bear strong sons, left her with a kiss
and flowed away. In time she had two boys
twin products of divine and mortal joys.

Next was Antiope, she too lay down
with an immortal - Zeus himself no less
and had two sons by him, both of renown.
They founded Thebes, city and high fortress.
Alcmene, who also slept with Zeus, met me
[that union had great Heracles as fruit]
His wife, Megara, was in her company.
I saw the mother of Oedipus, whose fate
was to marry her son; both unaware
until it was too late what they had done.
She hung herself, left him the guilt to bear
- that sin for which he never could atone
anchoring him with deep regret and shame
their sin commemorated in his name.

I saw the lovely Chloris, pale of skin
wife of Neleus; the princess Leda then
who was the mother of those fabled twins
Castor and Polydeuces [among men
both renowned] - one skilled in the boxing art
and his brother Castor who made his name
in taming headstrong horses. Never apart
in the womb, in death they were just the same.
Zeus honoured them as gods, let each one rise
on alternate days from death's dreamless rest
so that when each one is living, the other dies.
Leda also suckled at her breast
Helen of Troy and Clytemnestra too;
no women ever more famous than those two.

Iphimedeia now stood in line.
She'd mated with Poseidon, lord of sea
who surged inside her in the form of brine.
She had two sons out of this ecstasy:
at nine years old they towered to the sky
and threatened Olympus with thundering cries,
swearing they would destroy the gods on high.
Apollo, fearing that if they reached full size
they might not be beaten, brought them down,
these childish giants, with his unerring bow,
before their first faint manhood hair had grown
on those youngsters' chins. So pride was laid low,
those two upstarts, overgrown since birth,
reaching for the heavens, were brought back to earth.

Phaidra and Procris revealed themselves to me,
then Ariadnê, who with her ball of thread
saved Theseus from the maze, escaped by sea
with him. Sorrow, not joy, lay ahead.
She was killed by Artemis that same year.
Who else approached me from that line of shades?
Maera and Clymênê were also there
and evil Eriphylê who betrayed
her husband, seduced by the lure of gold.
How can I name them all - princesses, wives,
daughters, mothers - if everything was told
I would be telling you of countless lives
right through the night and dawn and into day
but must rejoin my crew, I cannot stay

Odysseus fell silent, then stared ahead
and for that moment not one sound was heard
from that enraptured crowd. Then Arête said
"Great Odysseus, what wonder have you stirred
within our hearts with your astounding tales?
Be assured of our hospitality
we'll stock your ship with gifts when your crew sails."
Echeneus, eldest in the company
agreed and king Alcinous gave command.
"Our friend longs for home and all gathered here
secure among their own, can understand
the call for home that resounds loud and clear
for weary wanderers. Stay one more day
to stock your ship before you sail away."

Odysseus addressed the king, bowing low
"I thank you for your hospitality
and will wait until you give me leave to go"
Alcinous smiled "Please tell our company
if you chanced to meet among the ranks of dead
any comrade who fought at Troy with you,
who fell there at your side? No need for bed
when our guest has tales, wonderful and true
to entertain us here throughout the night."
Odysseus answered him "It is my joy
to do what you request of me tonight.
I met the ghosts of friends who died at Troy
and some others, unharmed in grim warfare,
who came home to find sly death waiting there."

Once more Odysseus addressed the quiet crowd,
"Persephone, queen of the dead, then cleared
the womens' ghosts like wind clears drifting cloud.
The shade of Agamémnon now appeared
the son of Atreus, three friends at his side.
He sipped the blood and saw me standing there.
Tears welling in his eyes, the hero cried
and crossed to where I was. When he was near
he stretched his great arms so he might embrace
his old comrade but drifted like grey smoke
past my reaching hands. Tears streamed down my face
in pity for this warlord, and I spoke
"Did you meet death at sea or on dry land,
a cattle raid or combat hand to hand?"

"Odysseus, great tactician and good friend,
no battle on dry land, no storm at sea
but a heartless wife brought about my end,
helped by her lover. Cold blooded butchery!
They lured my friends and I with warmest words
to a homecoming feast, finest food and wine.
Then the killing started, sharp knives, sharp swords.
Food sated, we were slaughtered there like swine,
our slit throats bubbling, the floor a stream of blood.
My last sight was of Cassandra's piteous cry
as Clytaimnéstra moved to knife her. I stood
and with one final burst of energy
gripped her killing hand but the heartless whore
eluded me. I recall nothing more."

Agamémnon shook his head then said to me
"Never tell a woman all you know;
hold something in reserve. This mystery
will keep her patiently on leash. Although
my wife and I seemed close, flesh and fingernail,
she took my life. I see no such risk in sight
with your Penelope. When you set sail
she had a baby boy. If all is right
he must be a grown man by now; her support.
You will see him yet if the gods are kind.
My own wife, through either cruelty or sport
never let me see my son. Hold in mind
this warning now. Land your ship secretly
on Ithaca when you come home from sea."

"Land your ship in secret," he said once more
"Though Penelope seems loyal and true;
the days of faithful wives are days of yore.
But tell me now, before our time is through
what report of my dear son can you give?
Gone to Orchómenos or Pylos can he be
or with Meneláus in Sparta? He's alive
that much I know, or he'd stand here with me."
"Great Agamemnon" was all I could reply
"I have no news of him alive or dead
and empty words just cover up a lie"
He nodded solemnly and bowed his head
and moved away. His friends departed too.
I watched until they disappeared from view.

Next, I saw Patrocles in the crowd,
then Antilochus. Achilles grew near
and greeted me through tears, his manner cowed.
"O master tactician! What brings you here
to this dark place shrouded from mortal eyes,
where all the dim and fleshless dead reside?"
"I came to meet Tieresias the wise
to help me home - his prophecy my guide.
The gods have heaped misfortune on my head.
After years away, I'm still wandering
far from home while you rest among the dead.
Lord of this place as once you reigned as king
'till you fell at Troy, prime among your peers.
You are honoured here as well - why these tears?"

"Let me hear no sweet talk of death from you
Odysseus" he cried "I'd swop my place here
with some poor slave - do it willingly too,
if I could live again. But let me hear
news of my father, Peleus the brave.
Advanced in years, is he mistreated now
by Hellas and Phthia? Beyond the grave
what action could I take if that were so
in this my fleshless, boneless, bloodless state.
There's no turning back, my days of war are done."
"I know nothing of your father's fate
but can talk to you about your son
the prince Neoptólemos, your boy
who, like his father, made his name at Troy."

"Young and eager, he sailed under my command
out from Skyros to join our mighty fleet.
And I can tell you now, your son could stand
and hold his own in keen debate, defeat
all but Nestor and I in argument.
When we charged at the Trojan infantry
he never wilted in the ranks but spent
himself in every fight, the enemy
scattering before his raging red advance.
Scores went down before him as he charged through
with stabbing sword or with his trusted lance.
When those behind him stalled his courage grew
and led us on; but you had taught him well.
Now listen on, I have much more to tell."

"Your son was one of those I chose to hide
within the massive hollow horse with me.
It was built by Epeius and left outside
Troy's walls. I know that curiosity
would itch the Trojans and they proved me right.
The horse was wheeled inside the city walls
as spoils of war. In its belly we stayed quiet,
our heartbeats booming loud as waterfalls,
each man dreading that we might be found.
Later on, the Trojans celebrated;
raucous drinking in the streets, dancing round
our silent, wooden hatch. There we waited
'till they reeled to sleep, noise died on the air.
Now or never! The time to act was here."

"Gripping the trapdoor bolt to let us out
into the silent streets, I can recall
looking around; anxiety and doubt
on most faces there but not on all.
Your son was calm, a leader among peers,
all ready, for the bloody work ahead.
Among the seasoned fighters, twice his years,
he stood out in battle - the coolest head
of all our group when we attacked that night
the bravest too, right in the thick of things.
He was blessed in luck as well, in every fight
unmarked by the scars and wounds warfare brings."
Achilees nodded, moving from my side
when I had finished, his face lit up with pride.

Long lines of troubled dead approached me there
but one kept to himself, behind the crowd.
Ajax it was, watching with a brooding stare.
We had quarrelled over who should be allowed
the armour of Achilles and his weaponry
soon after that great hero had been killed
outside the walls of Troy - Ajax or me.
When the votes were cast, the assembly willed
they should be mine to keep. That judgement led
to Ajax' suicide, falling on his sword.
I gently called him, but he turned his head
and moved towards Erebos without a word,
so sorrowful and looking so alone.
I ran to follow him but he was gone.

Minos, son of Zeus, I saw nearby,
holding court and sitting on a throne
among ghostly pleaders. He lifted high
a golden staff at each judgement done.
I saw Orion, the hunter, draw near
gripping his bronze club, rounding up the same
wild beasts he'd overpowered without fear
before he died - his own herd now, not game.
Tityus, son of the goddess Earth lay tied
to nine square roods of earth, twisting in pain.
Vultures hunched above him on each side,
stabbing his belly time and time again.
Leto's rapist - this was the punishment
that Zeus had set, this unending torment.

I met three more shades, Tantalus was first,
trapped in a plashing pool up to his chin
in cool water, racked by a burning thirst.
No sooner did the parched old man begin
to move his lips towards the water there
than it disappeared, gulped back underground.
Fruit trees, fleeced with fig, pomegranate, pear,
cherry, apples, and olive all around,
but when the tyrant, maddened by hunger pain
reached to touch the luscious fruit overhead,
his desperate efforts proved to be in vain
as the laden boughs moved above his head.
Just desserts for this depraved, greedy one
who, asked to feed the gods, had served his son.

Sisyphus, arch master of trickery,
had fooled the lord of death, not once, but twice.
But Zeus punished this man's audacity;
for every mortal sin must have its price.
I saw this poor man, halfway up a hill
pushing a massive rock towards the crest
with all his strength of body and of will.
Right at the top, where he would pass the test
he had been set; his journey's end at hand,
the great boulder slipped out of his control,
bouncing back down the slope to level land.
So, he was doomed to start again, to roll
that crippling burden to the top once more
then face the same outcome that he'd faced before.

Next, I met the wraith of great Heracles.
Though this mighty hero resides among
the gods on high, his after-image stays
in this ghostly place, among the phantom throng.
The shades before him parted like wild fowl,
disturbed while feeding, startled into flight.
He looked so fierce, his face an angry scowl
with arrow notched to bow and bow strung tight.
He wore a golden belt, decorated
with pictures of savage lion, boar and bear,
and scenes of war, siege towns devastated
by sword and flame - his exploits all shown there.
The craftsman who made that belt would do well
never to repeat this depicted hell.

The great hero approached me and he said
"Odysseus. What chance brings you to this place
from sunlight to this kingdom of the dead?
Long ago I was ordered here to face
my toughest test - there were twelve in all;
Although a son of Zeus, it was my lot
to labour at the whim, the beck and call
of a master with temper quick and hot.
One final test he gave me was to track
dread Cerberus, that grim three headed hound
guarding this place and later take him back
- that brute's one time to leave the underground.
I did all that, but credit where credit's due,
Hera and Athena helped me too."

Though Heracles departed, I delayed
in case another hero came my way
like the mighty Theseus or the shade
of Peirithoos. But I did not stay
for a host of phantoms, dense as a cloud
of starlings swarming through the evening sky,
approached me there, a rustling whispering crowd.
I had a sense Persephone might try
to hold me there so quickly joined my crew.
We loosed the holding ropes and pulled from shore
each man rowing hard. Without more ado
we left that dismal place, exchanging oar
for stretched-out sail, filled by a helping wind
and soon had left that land of death behind.

Between two horrors

All day we sailed across the open sea
and as dusk set in, reached the quiet strand
on Aiais island, Circe's sanctuary.
Beneath the stars we slept on level sand.
Next day I sent a group of volunteers
to bring back the body of Elpênor
[among our crew the youngest one in years].
The rest of us climbed high above the shore
and cut down timbers there and burnt a pyre.
We stood by weeping as the flames burned through
his corpse and weaponry and when the fire
had done its work, his close friends among the crew
heaped up a mound and set his gravestone high;
placed his light, unwarped oar against the sky.

Soon after this queen Circe came our way
to celebrate our return from the dead.
She brought her handmaids, each one with a tray
bearing meat, ruby coloured wine and bread.
"It is the fate of mortals when death calls
that they go to Hades", the goddess cried
"with no return allowed from those dark halls.
But you have done all this yet have not died
and so will get to journey there once more
when your days are done. Rest and celebrate
with me before you set up sail or oar
for your voyage home. I will set you straight
with sailing routes and landmarks, you must chart.
One last night together, before we part."

Pleased by her offer, we did as she said
and feasted through that day and into night.
Knowing our long journey still stretched ahead
I felt my men deserved this brief respite.
Later as my shipmates slept on the shore,
Circe led me to a hidden cove
and lay beside me there; the ocean's roar
a backdrop to our swelling tide of love.
I told her then of all I'd seen and done
in the dark underworld, from first to last
since we'd mingled in her bed, two as one,
when she'd agreed to lift this spell she'd cast
on my poor shipmates, able bodied men,
each one a pig, imprisoned in her pen.

"Those trials are in the past", Circe said
as we lay in after-love, side by side.
"Listen carefully! There are trials ahead
when you leave this place. I will be your guide.
First in your path will be the Siren's call,
their honey voices are a tempting snare.
The poor sailor who changes his course in thrall
to their seductive sound is unaware
until it's far too late that he won't see
his family again, his own home place.
Their voices will wipe clear his memory
of all he ever loved. The only trace
of seamen who visit the Siren's land
is rolling flesh and bones heaped on a strand."

"To prevent this happening, heed me well.
Keep to open sea. Plug each crewman's ears
with beeswax kneaded soft to block the spell
before the coastline of the Sirens nears.
Reading your mind, I know you will decide
to listen to their captivating sound.
If that's your wish, order that you are tied
hand and foot to the mast, securely bound.
They must not free you, despite your threats or pleas
when you hear sweet voices from the shore.
They must ignore your cries that they release
you from the mast and straightaway ensure
more rope is wound around you as you cry
and stroke their oars until those voices die."

"If you come through that then you must decide
on one of two courses that you will face.
You must make this choice yourself - I can't guide
your hand on this, your judgement in advance,
but I can tell you now what lies ahead.
One route will take you out to cliffs that rear
almost touching the cloudbanks overhead.
Few birds can fly above them for their sheer
and glass smooth surface is a test too tough.
The doves that bring ambrosia in flight
to great Zeus above, plummet to the rough
and thundering seas below from that great height.
As one bird dies, Zeus, watching from above
sends at once another replacement dove!"

"And as for ships, so many capsized there,
churned up by boiling surf and flung by wind
against those lofty cliffs, so smooth and bare
that mooring ropes or grasping hands can't find
one crack or overhang as sanctuary,
against a desperate, drowning death below.
Strong craft end up as flotsam on the sea,
their crews as corpses. Just one ship we know
made that hazardous journey safely through.
That was the Argo, with Jason in command.
The divine Hera ensured that ship and crew
were saved. She had given a helping hand
out of love for Jason. All would have died
without the goddess Hera on their side."

"There is a second course that runs between
two dark headlands which you must journey by.
The summit of the first is never seen,
lost in stormcloud, grazing the very sky.
No man, even one with climbing expertise,
can scale this cliff face, rising smooth and sheer.
Halfway to the peak, facing on western seas,
lies a cavern, mist-shrouded through the year,
stretching towards Erebos, where the dead go.
This cave is set so high above the sea
that your best bowman from your ship below,
despite his proven skill in archery
could never shoot an arrow to that height –
his efforts falling short, try as he might!"

"Scylla lives in this den. Although her cry
is not much louder to the human ear
than a newborn pup's, she repels the eye;
a sight to inspire undiluted fear.
She has twelve legs like tentacles that wave
without joint or bone or nail in her wake.
Six long scrawny necks hold six heads above;
each head with triple row of fangs that break
through any creature's skin with fatal bite.
She lurks in her cave but her heads twist through
into outer air, checking from that height
on any dolphin, seal or passing crew.
No ship can get by her, she sweeps from each deck
six seafarers: one man for every neck."

"The other rock is lower and lies so near
the first headland across a narrow strait
that a bowshot would span the way. It's here
that the monster Charybdis lies in wait.
She turns into a whirlpool, fierce and fast,
sucking seawater down her massive throat
three times a day. Before the day has passed
she spews the water out three times: No boat
can escape her greedy appetite.
Take my advice and steer your ship away
from her hungry reach. Ensure you keep tight
by the cliff where Scylla lurks. In that way
you will only have to mourn six of your crew
instead of all your men and your ship too."

I am stubborn and had to talk this through.
"Could I not steer clear of Charybdis,
ward off Scylla and so protect my crew?"
Circe paused midway through a tender kiss
and smiled "You soldiers are all the same,
always spoiling for a fight", she replied,
"But fighting her is not a clever game.
You will perish as countless others died
who took on Scylla. Flight is your way out,
for by the time, you're ready to attack
with arrows notched to bowstrings, have no doubt,
Scylla will have pounced, swept six men from deck.
Speed by instead and call on the gods then
to stop a second strike or lose more men."

"Should you survive these trials, you will sail by
Thrinácia island, where sheep and cattle graze
owned by Helios, sun god of the sky.
Seven hundred creatures are there always
made up of seven flocks and seven herds.
They never die, no need of offspring here.
Immortal too their shepherds and cowherds
- Helios and Neaera their parents there.
Give these cows the widest berth. If you kill
one of this sacred herd your crew and craft
will be destroyed by rough seas then until
you arrive home - the one survivor left."
Circe was silent then and moved away
as dawn's rose light announced the start of day.

I woke the men, and we left straightaway
breaking the glassy sea with dipping blades.
Before we tired, kind Circe sent our way
a canvas filling breeze, so my comrades
raised our sails, letting the helmsman and the wind
move our ship. I spoke to all the crew
"Friends! Circe has foretold what we will find
ahead and has advised us what to do.
We are to shun the Sirens' song or die
instead, Circe the great queen has forecast
I alone may listen so you must tie
me up, tight as a splint against the mast.
If I should shout or beg to be set free
whatever you may do, do not heed me."

The men agreed and we sped on our way,
but as we neared the Sirens' territory
our driving wind abruptly died away
leaving stillness in the air and becalmed sea.
So, we furled up sail and began to row
and as my shipmates sculled with practiced skill,
I took a cake of beeswax from below
a rowing bench and carved at it until
I had fashioned ear stops for all the crew.
I rolled them in my hand when this was done
to soften them [an easy thing to do
as Helios sent a burning midday sun
to speed my work] and when the coast drew near
I gathered my men, plugged up every ear.

They tied me up securely to the mast
then sat down again, each man at his oar.
We came within hailing distance of the coast
where the two Sirens, watching from the shore,
broke into bewitching song straight away.
"Drop your anchor Odysseus and draw near
to hear our voices! No one who comes our way
journeys past this spot without giving ear
to our sweet tones." I struggled to be free
shouting, twisting my head from side to side
but my shipmates rowed on, ignoring me.
Then Perimêdês and Eurylochus tied
more rope around my waist and kept me there
until the Sirens' song died on the air.

My crew unblocked their ears then set me free
from all my bonds. Just then, out of the blue,
gigantic breakers loomed across the sea
towards our frail craft. Seeing this, the crew
were terrified and oars were dropped from hands
leaving us drifting towards that massive swell.
That was the time, I knew to take command.
So, I addressed those men I knew so well
"We have come through far more than this" I cried
"So, take heart, my friends. I came to your aid
not too long ago. You were trapped inside
the Cyclops' cave bewildered and afraid.
I led you out of there, so have no fear;
I'll also lead you through this danger here."

"So, heads up lads and let's give this our best;
grab your oar blades and row without delay
towards that rocky headband to the west."
Thus, I rallied them, and straightaway
we were on the move again, hope restored.
As the cliff where Scylla waited drew near
I was worried, but didn't say a word
in case my crew again succumbed to fear
and dropped their oars as they had done before.
I tied on armour, then, with spear in hand
stood on the foredeck as the ship neared shore
to see the monster, determined to stand,
no matter what the chances were, and fight
despite Circe's warning the other night.

Without delay we rowed into the strait
Scylla to port and on the starboard side
Charybdis - two monsters lying in wait.
My shipmates [all brave men] were terrified
when they saw Charybdis gape ahead.
As she vomited, sea water was thrown
in streaming plumes to the cliffs overhead,
which, at the summit, suddenly fell down
as torrential rain. When she swallowed whole
that mass of falling water we could see
the inner vortex, hear the thunder roll
of rock and dark sea sand churned violently
out of the seabed. Amazed by this sight,
we watched that yawning mouth in utter fright.

Like a striking snake, out of nowhere,
Scylla pounced, snatching six of my crew
up from the deck and swing them into air.
I saw their dangling arms and legs and knew
I would never see them alive once more.
I heard them call my name with shrieks and shouts.
Just like an angler, fishing from the shore
for mackerel, having dropped the hooked bait out,
will rip fish from the surface of the sea
so, Scylla jerked my friends up to her den
and ate them there, then reached back down for me.
Of all that I've seen in the world of men
that was the worst. We rowed, powered by fright
until those grim headlands were out of sight.

We neared the sun god's isle. Still out at sea
we could hear the sounds, carried on the wind,
of his well-fed sheep and cows. Suddenly
Tieresias' warning came to my mind
and Circe's also. So, I told my crew
of these two prophecies. "Let's pull away
from this place as we have been told to do."
Cursing me, Eurylochus had his say
"Odysseus! Are you flesh and blood at all?
Do you never tire? Here we are, half dead
sleepy on our oars. Night is set to fall.
Let us go ashore at once to make our bed
on solid ground and eat our supper there.
We'll rise at dawn and sail away from here."

Now when the rest agreed with him, I knew
I was outmatched. I said "I will agree
if a solemn oath is sworn by all crew
that any grazing cow or sheep we see
will stay unharmed during our visit there.
We'll make do instead with Circe's generous store."
The men seemed satisfied, but I took care
to stand and listen as each shipmate swore.
So, we moored the ship on a halfmoon strand
with cool and bubbling water springs nearby.
When we had dined, we gathered on the sand
and mourned our friends we'd seen so cruelly die;
a death so undeserved by those good men,
devoured, before our eyes, in Scylla's den.

Now as we slept, great Zeus unleashed a gale
with pitch black clouds shrouding land and sea.
When we woke; we know to try to sail
on such rough water would be lunacy
so, we dragged our ship farther up the strand.
I repeated my warning to the crew
"The cattle and the sheep on this island
belong to Helios and we will rue
the day that any one of them is killed.
We have sufficient food and drink on board,
our hold is groaning with provisions filled
by Circe." Yet again they gave their word.
All seemed settled and yet my heart was sore,
wondering what other trials Zeus had in store.

I sensed danger and that's how things worked out,
for we were trapped there longer than we planned
by savage storms that raged day in day out
for one full month, stirred up by Zeus' hand.
Soon all the food store in the hold was gone
and hunger drove the crew to scour the shore
with hooks, then inland with their spears for game.
As these lean days dragged on, the men grew sore
in manner; fights and arguments each day.
And still the storms raged on without respite.
One morning I withdrew from them to pray
to the gods for delivery from our plight.
I found a sheltered spot, washed my hands there
then fell asleep as I finished prayer.

Meanwhile, behind my back, as I slept there,
Eurylochus assembled all my crew.
"Friends" he said "We've endured more than our share
of hardship, but famine is something new:
some say the worst of deaths for mortal men.
Right beside us here is the remedy;
well fed cattle. Let's slaughter some and then
sacrifice to the gods who own the sky.
As well as that, when we get home some day
we'll build a temple filled with offerings.
Should Helios flare up now and make us pay
by sinking us as sea, that's a better thing
than this wasting away and withering down
to skin and bone. For myself, I'd rather drown!"

They all agreed with him and straight away
trooped to where prime cattle grazed inland.
They stood around the chosen beasts to pray,
scattering oak leaves [no barley being at hand]
on the heifers' heads with due ceremony
before their throats were cut. When this was complete
the thighbones, wrapped in fat, were all carved free
and laid upon a fire with strips of meat.
As libation, they used water from a spring
and broiled the entrails first – having no wine.
When they had burnt their ritual offering
they roasted prime cuts and sat down to dine
on the spitted meat, wolfing down each bite
and ate, until they'd satisfied their appetite.

Just then I woke. As I retraced my way,
I caught the waft of cooked meat on the air.
I cried aloud in anger and dismay
"Great Zeus, in high Olympus. It's not fair
you left me sleeping while such deeds were done!"
Meanwhile, Lampetie, that quick messenger,
brought news to Helios, lord of the sun,
of what had taken place. In his anger
he sought restitution or penalty
to be witnessed by the gods on high.
He warned if Olympus did not agree
he would withdraw the sun, drop it from the sky
leaving earth to freeze. He would shine instead
in the underworld, dark realm of the dead.

Zeus listened to Helios and made reply
"There is no need to make all mortals pay
for the deeds of one small group. From the sky
I will throw one white hot bolt on the day
they set sail again and blast their ship
to splinters and let every crewman drown."
I heard this later from Calypso's lips
[she was told by Hermes when he came down
to force her hand so I could be let go
from her loving bonds.] I rejoined my crew
and faced each man and let my anger show
but it was far too late. What could I do?
The cows were butchered. The deed was done.
No remedy – this could not be undone.

For six full days my crew were glad to eat
prime beef despite grim portents from above
sent to warn us: both raw and roasted meat
lowed like living cows; hides began to move.
Then Zeus stepped in and caused the storm to cease,
granting us our chance to leave at last.
So, we boarded our ship and with an offshore breeze
moved away from land, travelling true and fast.
Then a dark cloud loomed in front, out of the blue,
steered by Zeus, poised directly overhead –
and then, to the amazement of the crew,
the sea around the boat grew dark as lead.
We moved on, each man working at his oar,
each one eager to reach our native shore.

We held our course but suddenly a gale
struck with savage force, whining from the west
across our moving craft, ripping the sail
out on the churned-up sea, toppling the mast
down on our deck, felling our steersman there.
It pitched him in the sea with caved in skull.
Now with thunder crack through the darkened air
Zeus let fly a bolt which struck the hull
a direct hit with a sulphur after smell.
All my shipmates were flung into the sea
with each man drowning in the savage swell.
I clutched at a spar that had broken free
and climbed on it, despite the ocean's force;
a rider on a buckling, untamed horse.

Worse was to come! A sudden change of wind
swept me northwards, still clinging to the post.
Next day, the place I thought I'd left behind
came into view; that accursed coast
where Charybdis and Scylla lurked. I could see
Charybdis, all gaping wide, straight ahead
but I leaped upwards to that great fig tree
hung there like a bat as waters sped
into that raging vortex and clung tight
knowing what had been swallowed would reappear.
And sure enough [it was a welcome sight!]
my board re-emerged at last. I jumped clear
into the bubbling foam and pulled astride,
rowing with both my hands against the tide.

Odysseus lands in Ithaca

I paddled on as quickly as I could
in dread that Scylla might now appear
and snatch me off my bobbing length of wood.
Zeus must have taken pity on my fear
and kept me from that brutal monster's hands.
Once through the strait and out on open sea,
I drifted for nine days and then made land
on Calypso's shore. The nymph welcomed me
with outmost hospitality and grace
into her house and soon into her heart.
Soon I became a prisoner in that place
surrounded by the sea, remote, apart.
But you have heard that story here last night
to repeat it now would be impolite.

When Odysseus finished, the hall went still
until King Alcinous turned to his guest
"My friend, you will not leave this place until
my servants have fully packed your farewell chest
with gold, clothing, and precious jewellery.
You will take a tripod on board with you
and a cauldron. I promise this assembly
and these clansmen know my word is true,
to recoup the cost of this farewell store
from our own people to make our burden light"
They all approved the King's plan with a roar.
Next day the treasure was stowed, packed in tight
under the rowing benches of the ship
and all arrangements were made for the trip.

This done, they all returned to drink and dine,
a farewell banquet in the royal hall.
Alcinous slew an ox and poured red wine
to honour Zeus. The king then turned to call
Demodocus, the blind harper, to play.
Only Odysseus, anxious and heart sore
turned his head to face the sunset on the bay,
impatient for the open sea once more,
just like a ploughman, labouring without rest
behind his team of oxen and ploughshare
savours the dipping sunlight in the west
- a sign his work is done. And now, aware
that he must choose his words quite carefully,
Odysseus stood and made a heartfelt plea.

"My blessing on you all in this great court,
I am thankful for all you've done for me;
a ship all rigged and ready in your port
to bring this stranger home across the sea
with fine treasure that you have stowed on board.
It is my wish to sail away tonight
to end my long exile and be restored
as lord of Ithaca. My heart's delight
will be to see, after long and lonely years,
my wife and son who must assume I'm dead.
Bring me home this night!" His eyes filled with tears
and all listening were moved by what he said.
King Alcinous now stood, wine bowl in hand
and requested that everyone should stand.

The king beckoned his squire and spoke to him.
"Pontonous" he said "Ensure that you fill
each goblet for a toast right to the brim."
When all was done according to his will
Alcinous rose to his feet and spoke once more.
"May great Zeus bless us all and speed our guest
safely across the sea to his own shore."
When all assembled there had drunk the toast,
Odysseus took his bowl and gently set
it in Arete's hand and bowed his head.
"Farewell great Queen, this wanderer won't forget
the kindness you have shown him here" he said
"To your husband and yourself I bid goodbye,
may you both be blessed by the gods on high."

Odysseus turned away and strode outside
the royal court to where the ship was moored
with the kind's herald at his right-hand side.
Arete sent her maids along, who stored
clothing, food and wine and the treasure chest
under the benches. They prepared a bed
in the after deck where Odysseus might rest.
When he climbed aboard, he laid his head
and heedless of the noise of work, fell asleep.
Meanwhile the crew pulled quickly from the shore
then past the harbour walls into the deep.
Each man, though working on a separate oar
dipped his blade in perfect unison
with his comrades, all moving as one.

As they sailed, their passenger, unaware
slept deep and dreamless. He, who for twenty years
faced trials in skirmishes and brute warfare
on land and sea- a hero among peers
slept serenely on board the bucking ship.
Like a four horse team who wait impatiently
to surge ahead at the first touch of the whip
so ran that craft, riding across the sea.
Right through the night she arrowed on her way,
faster than a falcon in downwind flight
[the fastest of all sea birds so they say]
and reached Ithaca in dawn's rose coloured light.
They chose a sheltered cave in which to land
and with careful skill eased her up on sand.

The sailors know this cove, had been before.
It was the perfect place, a hidden bay
to leave Odysseus with his treasure store.
As soon as they had put their oars away,
they carried their passenger, still asleep,
and placed him on dry sand past reach of sea.
They laid the treasure then into a heap
at the foot of a mighty olive tree,
then climbed on board and rowed away again.
But now Poseidon, watching from on high,
approached his brother Zeus to complain.
"As gods, we lose respect when mortals fly
in the face of what we would have them do;
respect lost on earth and on Olympus too."

"The Phaeacians have ignored my will", he cried,
"By helping Odysseus in such a way,
ensuring his every need was supplied,
an honoured guest on an extended stay.
Now, rubbing salt into the wound, they bring
him home to Ithaca in their own ship
laden with gifts from their own queen and king.
I need to teach these upstarts, crack the whip.
I'll sink them as they sail back home again.
When that is done, I will fence their town
with a ring of mountains, a rocky chain
to stop them seafaring, keep them pinned down.
No more escorting travellers on the sea,
they'll rue the disrespect they have shown me."

"My brother" said Zeus "let this ship return
but when those gathered, watching from the pier
can see her nearing port, then we will turn
that boat to stone. A ship shaped island there
where once a vessel moved across the sea!
Men will gape at this amazing sight
for generations to come. It will be
a stark reminder that mortals cannot fight
the will of gods. But there's no need to throw
a ring of mountains down to block their port.
You are the lord of seas, and you should know
there's no useful purpose there. We'll get sport
and satisfaction from this trick alone;
this reprimand from Olympus set in stone."

When Zeus finished, Poseidon made his way
to Scherie where the Phaeacians live,
and saw the vessel making good headway
towards the port. Before it could arrive
he drew near. With one palm slap of his hand
he turned her into stone and left the scene.
The welcome party watching from the land
were shocked; could not believe what they'd seen.
They turned to King Alcinous who replied
"This makes sense of my father's prophecy
that Poseidon would punish our people's pride
in treating those who are shipwrecked at sea
as honoured guests – as if they were our own
and ensuring them a safe escort home."

"Listen my people! Our customs now must change
to avoid divine punishment again.
My father also said a mountain range
would fence our city in its rocky chain
unless we are seen to change our ways.
As for the present, let's select with care
twelve bulls as sacrifice and sing due praise
to the great sea god and ask him to spare
our city, which depends upon the sea,
from being landlocked by mountains all around."
This they set to do immediately
assembling on ceremonial ground
led by their king. This sacrificial rite
they hoped was pleasing in Poseidon's sight.

Meanwhile Odysseus woke but could not tell
what land it was – Athena had disguised
his long-sought homeland, Ithaca, so well
it was now an unknown place to his eyes.
She also hid him in a sacred screen
to ensure, that as he moved from place to place,
he could see around him but not be seen.
She did all this so none might see his face:
suitors, his own townsmen, or family.
And so, confused, he looked around and swore,
slapping his thighs with both hands repeatedly.
"Why have they dropped me on this foreign shore
when they had promised me that I would land
on Ithaca? I cannot understand."

"How will I find my way without a guide
to steer my steps? What is to be done
with this heaped up treasure; where can I hide
it safely? Out in the open anyone
who spots it would steal it straightaway.
Lord Alcinous and his men were not true,
leaving me in this strange place. I will pray
to Zeus above to punish that sly crew!
But first I must go through this treasure trove
and check to see if everything is there.
Who's to know they were to remove
the richest things and leave the others here?"
Odysseus checked it out but everything
was in place, as directed by the king.

Not knowing he was on his native shore,
Odysseus, worn from wandering, now cried.
Athena came, as she had done before
in a young man's form, to stand by his side.
Odysseus took heart from this company.
"My friend, you are the first one I have seen
since I landed here. Can you inform me
the nature of this place – by which I mean
is this an island or a mainland coast,
and what name do the natives call this place?"
Athena smiled. "Stranger, you must be lost
far from your home or maybe it's the case
that you are a fool not to know the name
of this land, well deserving of its fame."

"Although there is a lack of meadows here
for training horses, the soil is very fine
and yields generous crops of corn each year.
Its vineyards produce the very best of wine,
this place has pasturelands and forests too.
All in all, the name Ithaca is known
as far away as Troy, let me tell you."
Odysseus kept his face as set as stone
though inwardly his heard was beating fast
to hear he was in Ithaca again.
He answered now, as often in the past,
with clever words, designed to explain
his presence and the treasure at his side.
So, without hesitation, he replied.

"Ithaca! I have heard that name before,
from as far away as Crete, my homeland.
With half my fortune, I've landed on this shore,
the rest is left to my children. Here I stand,
an exile for a murder I carried out.
I killed Orsilochus, the best athlete
in our country without a single doubt.
My Trojan booty I had brought to Crete
[just reward for service on the battlefield]
he planned to steal. Another motive here
during Troy's siege, I had refused to yield
to his father as my commander there,
preferring to lead men in that great fight
than serving under him – I was proved right."

"I had to snuff his threat, so acted fast
and set up ambush, accompanied by a friend.
We waited at a place he would go past
to come home at a narrow roadside bend.
As he approached, with one unerring throw,
I pinned my bronze bladed spear through his throat.
I thought it safer then to up and go
and paid for passage on a merchant boat
out of my treasure trove from Troy. The crew
agreed to set me down without delay
in Pylos or Elis, but strong gales blew,
driving us way off course here to this bay.
They placed me sleeping on the sand, my gear
stacked close beside me and then sailed from here."

Now before Odysseus' astonished eyes,
Athena stood, lovely in form and face,
where the young man had stood before, disguise
discarded, then turned to him with smiling face.
"No mortal can match your ingenuity
so godlike in its range. That skill we share.
On Olympus, among my family
I'm the god famous for fast thinking there.
And yet for all your guile, you are so slow,
not seeing that I'm always at your side.
It was I who urged King Alcinous to show
you kindness. Now, I'm here again to hide
your treasure trove which lies in open view
and then to give advice what you must do."

"You must not tell a single person here
that you are back from all your wandering.
Let patience be your guide; accept with cheer
the slights and indignities that men will fling
in your face, not realising who you are."
Odysseus turned to her, and he replied,
choosing his words with customary care.
"It's true that years ago you took my side
outside the Trojan walls, that tough campaign.
But since then, you have left me to my fate;
the two of us have never met again
until that time at Lord Alcinous' gate.
Tell me the truth – this shore on which I stand:
is this Ithaca or some other land?"

"Though I've told you this is Ithaca, I see
no rush on you to meet your kith and kin.
Unlike most travellers long away at sea,
you seek no news as to how your wife has been.
Instead, you seem intent on checking out
her faithfulness while you have been away.
Let me tell you; there is no cause to doubt
her on that score. She hungered night and day
through those lonely years to see you once again.
I always knew that you would make it through.
As for deserting you, let me explain.
My uncle, Lord Poseidon, hated you
and vowed revenge. Out of respect, not fear,
I stood back at times, did not interfere."

Athena stretched out her arms and made clear
what she had hidden from Odysseus' sight.
Lord Phorcy's cove; Mount Neion rising sheer,
fleeced with forest, lit up by evening light;
the sea nymph's cave, the long-leaved olive tree
above the entrance to the inner bay.
Odysseus kissed the ground now he could see
it was his native soil. Without delay
he stored his treasure trove inside the cave
while Athena sealed the entrance with a rock.
And now the two sat in a nearby grove
under shade, with Odysseus still in shock
that he was home. But much work lay ahead
Athena knew, she turned to him and said.

"Oh, son of Laertes, you must find a way
to rid vile suitors who for three whole years
have camped in your own household, These vultures' prey
on your wife who, with patience, guile and tears
keeps them at arm's length as she waits for you."
At this Odysseus said. "I might have died,
like King Agamemnon did who never knew
the death that lay in wait at his fireside
when he returned home from the Trojan fight!
Oh grey eyed goddess, help me out once more;
together we can put this crew to flight.
I'd face three hundred suitors, even four;
teach them lessons for everyone to see
if I knew Athena was helping me."

"Yes, I will help your cause," Athena said
"And will be there with you. I can foresee
the hall floor of your castle running red
with their blood. Take this as my prophecy.
But now to work! I will cast a spell
and wither your smooth skin, then turn your hair
to grey, exchange your clothes for rags that smell
so that those who meet you are unaware
of your identity. Now you must go
to see your loyal swineherd straight away
and ask him everything you want to know.
I will go to Sparta without delay
to bring your son, to join us in your fight,
restoring your good name and his birth right."

In the Swineherd's Hut

"You knew I was alive and could have set
my son at ease from needless doubt and fear?"
Odysseus asked. "No need to fret"
Athena answered. "I was always near
his side as he sailed seeking news of you.
I also know the suitors lie in wait
to ambush him but that scheming crew
will not succeed, for let me tell you straight
their doom is sealed; your son won't come to harm."
Athena touched her wand on Odysseus' head
shrivelling the smooth skin of his legs and arms,
and made his hair fall out, his fine eyes shed
their light – an old man now! When this was done
she left at once to find Odysseus' son.

When she was gone, Odysseus, staff in hand,
carrying a knapsack held by a shoulder strap,
set out along the trail to higher ground.
Soon he found the place, perched on a hilltop,
fenced in by a stockade, built strong and high.
The swineherd's hut and twelve sties were built inside
where six hundred sows, fifty to each sty
were safely penned. The boars remained outside,
guarded by four dogs, each one a savage beast.
The swineherd had to kill one fatted boar
every day for the raucous suitor's feast.
He was sitting beside his own porch door
with a leather strip, shaping with a blade,
a pair of sandals, working under shade.

As Odysseus approached the stockade wall,
the guard dogs rushed at him, a snarling pack.
He squatted down at once, let his staff fall.
Even so, they were eager to attack
this ragged stranger who had chanced their way
had not the swineherd jumped up with a shout
and threw stones to distract them from their prey.
"The gods are on your side, no doubt
that you've escaped them more or less intact.
If you'd been bitten here, I'd be to blame;
one more problem to join the others stacked
at my door! My master's gone. To my shame
I'm forced to kill and send to court my hogs
to feed suitors there, rougher than those dogs."

"My master's gone, none know his whereabouts,
he could be starving far away from here
while I feed his prize hogs to greedy louts.
Come to my hut, I am anxious to hear
your name and history." He led the way
to the hut and beckoned Odysseus in.
He heaped up brushwood there, on this he lay
his own mattress, a shaggy wild goat's skin,
making a cosy sofa for his guest.
Odysseus thanked him for this courtesy.
The swineherd said "Beggars are a test
Zeus sets to mark man's hospitality.
You are welcome to anything I own
it isn't much but make yourself at home."

"My name is Eumaeus" the swineherd said
"Living in poverty, neglected here
since my good master left – he must be dead
according to the rumours that I hear.
He was generous; would have seen me right
given me a wife, cottage, fields to till
to reward my service, but sailed to fight
for Helen, on whose account blood would spill
and countless lives would be cast away."
Eumaeus went quiet and strode outside
to choose two young porkers then straightaway
he slaughtered them, then singed and flayed each hide.
He quartered them before he cooked the meat,
then sliced the pork for Odysseus to eat.

"Those suckling pigs are all I can offer you
as the prize hogs are slaughtered day and night
for suitors who act as if they knew
my master's dead. They think they have the right
to stalk his wife and feast at his expense,
while gulping down his cellar's finest wine.
Good thing my master's assets are immense;
great flocks of sheep, twelve herds of cows and swine
and goats. From these, each and every single day
animals are killed to keep those bastards fed!"
Odysseus listened in anger and dismay
but kept control. Eventually he said
"Who's your master? I've journeyed all my life
and may have news about him for his wife."

"Let me tell you" Eumaeus replied
"His lady and his son will turn deaf ears
to rumours. Many wandering men have lied
in return for rest and food through the years.
Each one tells my mistress a pretty tale
to raise false hopes then leaves her all distressed.
I well suppose that you too could regale
her eager ears but hear me out, my guest.
My lord is dead! His bones lie strewn on land
or buried or else picked clean in the sea.
I miss his kindness, his firm guiding hand
as I miss my parents [I pray I'll see
them both in the underworld, someday]
Odysseus, my master – He's dead, I say."

Odysseus nodded, then he spoke again.
"My friend", he said, "your master will return.
I swear to that. Don't ask me to explain.
I will accept any reward I earn
for this good news only when he comes home.
You can dress me then in due finery.
This will all take place; let it be known
your master will return here, you will see
within two moons – the waning of the old
and well before the waxing of the new.
And now, remember this – you have been told
he will gain vengeance on this heartless crew
who mistreat his loyal wife and his son.
I swear on all of this – It will be done."

"That reward will never be paid out
old man. Even though it would give me joy
to see Odysseus, let there be no doubt
that he is dead. Now it is his boy
Telemachus for whom we have to fear.
Someone, god or man, made the youngster rush
to Pylos for news of his father there.
The suitors plan to kill him; an ambush
on his voyage home. They will lay in wait
near Asteris. May Zeus keep him from harm.
Enough of that! Now let your words be straight
and true – you're a welcome guest to my farm
but guests bring news – as a fee for their stay
- a painless cost I'm sure that you will pay."

"So, tell me now – I am eager to hear.
Who are you? Where's your home and family?
What kind of ship – whose sailors brought you here?
I don't suppose you walked here on the sea!"
Odysseus replied, thinking on his feet
"My mother was a slave who shared her bed
with Castor, a rich man who lived in Crete.
To his credit, he lavished on my head
the love and care his own wife's son was shown.
When after long illness he passed away
his sons rose up against me. I was thrown
a pittance, given a meagre home to stay.
But I was a clever man; improved my life
and took a wealthy heiress as my wife."

"Looking at me now, frail and infirm,
I'm a shell of the man I used to be.
My love was warfare. I was stout in arm
and courage, fighting on land or on sea.
I never cared for farming and stayed clear
from domestic life, relishing the thrill
of carnage, the brute work of lance and spear.
I led my men on raiding trips until
I grew wealthy, respected throughout Crete.
I played my part in sacking Troy's proud walls
and arrived home safely, although our fleet
was scattered by the gods. But soon the call
of action made me restless and heart sore:
barely back from battle, hungry for more."

"And so, I rigged nine ships and gathered round
a crew. We offered sacrifice and prayer
to the gods then sailed away, Egypt bound.
Thanks to a fresh north wind we landed there,
at the Nile's flat delta on the fifth day.
I sent patrols to check and report back,
but reckless greed led them all astray.
There and then they proceeded to attack
a farming settlement – an easy raid;
enslaving the women and the children too
then putting all the men there to the blade.
But someone, somehow got a message through
to a nearby town and by morning light
their army had besieged us, primed to fight."

"At dawn they pounced, attacking our small band.
My men were overwhelmed, transfixed by dread,
greatly outnumbered in an unfamiliar land.
I saw good friends of mine among our dead
and others carried into slavery.
As for myself, I threw away my shield
my helmet and my spear then bent my knee
before their king and tearfully appealed
to him to spare my life. Zeus heard my prayer
for the king, so moved by my heartfelt tears
placed me in his chariot and drove from there
to his royal court. For seven happy years
I stayed there; became the king's trusted friend.
I grew rich but all that came to an end."

"Being careful with your choice of company
was a lesson that I learned to my woe.
I met a man, well versed in trickery
who persuaded me that he and I should go
to Phoenicia which was his native land.
I stayed there for a year on his estate
before he suggested that I lend a hand
on a trip to Libya, transporting freight.
Although I sensed he had a scheme in mind
to sell me as a slave when we got there
I agreed with this, hoping I might find
a way to catch the bastard unaware;
throw him overboard [not too hard to do]
and steer for home first having bribed the crew."

"Men make plans, but gods have their own plans too.
Our ship set sail, was soon on open sea
when Zeus struck, sending bolts of lightning through
the centre of the vessel – I could see
the scorch marks all along the deck and mast.
Sulphur reeked the air – that sharp sour smell
as men were flung overboard with the blast,
floating first, then drowning in the swell.
I was saved; some god came to my aid,
sending the toppled mastpole to my side.
I coiled myself around it, somehow stayed
afloat despite the howling gales that tried
to sink me. On the tenth day I made land
a great roller washed me, half dead, on to sand."

"I'd beached on Thesprotia, a land
ruled by Pheidon, a wise big hearted king.
His own son found me half dead on the sand
and brought me to the court. May great Zeus bring
him long life for his kindness and his care.
The king informed me of another guest,
Odysseus, who had recently stayed there.
This man had left a bulging treasure chest
while he was gone to check the gods' decree
at Dodona – should he sail home on the quiet
to Ithaca or return openly?
Meanwhile the king, taking pity on my plight
now ordered that a vessel be prepared
to bring me home but cruel fate interfered."

"As we left port the crew surrounded me
dressed me in rags and tied me to a bench,
hoping to sell me into slavery.
They anchored up coast from here, at a beach
and disembarked to eat their supper there.
I pried the ropes loose 'till they fell away,
wound the rags around my head and then swam clear
with quiet and steady strokes across the bay.
They returned to ship when their meal was done
and searched for me but to no avail.
I hid in undergrowth 'till they were gone
back on board the vessel and had set sail
then put my rags back on. Thus, poorly dressed
I journeyed through the night – you know the rest."

"You had my sympathy", the swineherd said
"till you spoke of Odysseus living yet.
That's total nonsense as the man is dead.
For reasons of their own the gods didn't let
him die in glory on Troy's battleground
or at home where his friends and family
would have raised a fitting funeral mound.
Last year another man tried fooling me
saying Odysseus had been seen in Crete
with Idomeneus, ruler of that place.
His was busy, repairing his own fleet
this trickster claimed, staring me in the face.
He told me Odysseus would soon set sail
with full crew and treasure chest, without fail."

"That man was a trickster. Now you come by
trading rumours for shelter, food and drink."
With cunning words Odysseus made reply
"You are a most suspicious man, I think,
but let us make a bargain here today.
If soon you see your master in this place
you will reward me – let's agree the way
- a new shirt and cloak! But if it's the case
that your master Odysseus fails to appear
let your men throw me from a cliff, a sign
to warn any other rogue who comes here.
Let's make this pledge and toast it now with wine."
The swineherd smiled. "Let's put that thought to rest
I will not undertake to kill a guest."

Outside they heard pigs squealing, drover's cries
as the herd was rounded up at close of day
and herded from the fields into their sties,
then penned there for the night. Without delay
the swineherd killed a fattened boar – one of his best,
so that all who worked there could eat and drink
in honour of their unexpected guest.
"Lads! It's time we enjoyed ourselves, I think"
the swineherd cried "Working from dawn to night
to feed those suitors for no pay or praise."
There and then when due sacrificial rite
to all the gods had been observed, piled trays
of fine wine and bread and choice cuts of meat
were brought to Odysseus for him to eat.

As night drew in, with driving wind and rain
Odysseus, dressed in rags, was feeling chill
and so decided to test once again
his host's compassion. He chose his words with skill.
"With wine, the quietest man may sing or cry
or tell a tale that might be best untold.
Laying an ambush near the walls of Troy
great Odysseus and Menelaus enrolled
me to lead the group with them – third in command!
When we came close to the brooding city wall
we crouched on boggy reed-infested land.
The wind dropped off and sleet began to fall,
whitening our shields. All our company
had cloaks to keep them warm, except for me."

"When I couldn't stand the cold any more
I nudged Odysseus who lay next to me.
"Son of Laertes, I'm frozen to the core
without a cloak. I swear that I won't see
the morning without extra clothes to wear."
Quick as a flash, he told me to be quiet
then called out to the rest. "Lads, listen here
I've had a warning dream – before this night
is done we must get a message through
to Agamemnon that he needs to send
extra troops to us here." Without ado
young Thoas threw off his cloak on the ground
and raced towards the camp. Meanwhile I lay
warm inside the cloak he'd flung away!"

"Your story is well told, its meaning clear"
the swineherd said. "Tonight, you'll be kept warm
with extra bedclothes there is no need to fear
on that account. But on our simple farm
we have no surplus clothes; each man here has one
cloak to wear for work. However, who knows,
you may be favoured by Odysseus' son
[should he return] with presents of fine clothes?"
The swineherd then prepared a cosy bed
for his guest. This being done, he left him there
went into the night, covering his head
against the wind, taking with him a spear
to guard the herd. Odysseus was moved to see
this man's care for his absent lord's property.

Telemachus Returns

Meanwhile Pallas Athena sped her way
to the court of Menelaus to advise
Odysseus' son that he should not delay
in returning home. She used no disguise
this time, standing tall by the young man's bed
as he tossed restlessly, eyes full of tears
for his missing father whom he feared dead.
"Rise, cast off your bedclothes and your fears"
the goddess urged. "Go to your mother's side.
It seems as if all the suitors have agreed
that she should become Eurymachus' bride.
It is likely that he will act in greed,
take as dowry all your belongings too.
Listen, and I will tell you what to do."

"When you return – and do that straightaway,
leave your goods with a trusted servant there.
Listen now, and do exactly as I say;
the suitors have an ambush set, a snare
in place near Same with your death in mind.
When you reach that coast, steer well east of land
[someone immortal will help to change the wind].
After that, step ashore at the first strand,
but send your ship and crew to the next port,
while you go inland to the swineherd's farm,
your father's friend. Let this man report
that you are safely home. This news will arm
your mother with hope". Fading out of sight,
Athena disappeared into the night.

When she left, Telemachus roused his friend,
Prince Peisistratus from soft depths of sleep.
"Wake up – our visit here is at an end.
We need to leave at once! "All will keep"
yawned Nestor's son, "it is too dark outside
and if we leave with such indecent speed
Lord Menelaus, our host, will be denied
the chance to bid us farewell or indeed
to give us parting gifts. A guest holds dear
the memory of any kindness shown.
Our leaving now would be a snub, I fear,
to our kind host. Leave well enough alone
until daylight comes for it isn't right
to slip away like two thieves in the night."

At crack of dawn the two young princes woke
and joined the king when he had left his bed.
Telemachus bowed low and then he spoke
"My lord, I'm longing to be home". he said,
Menelaus of the war cry then replied
"I won't keep you if that us your request.
As with all things, moderation is our guide.
It's very wrong to rush away a guest
who would like to stay and wrong to cling
to guests when they're in haste to be away.
Give me time to gather gifts, my offering
to you on your journey home today.
But first of all, young men, let us break bread,
a breakfast meal for the road ahead."

"If on the other hand you chose to wait
a few more days I'll take the two of you
on a trip; moving from this city gate
to Hellas and the Argive country too,
Each of the lords out there will gift you gold
or bronze artefacts or a pair of mules."
Telemachus answered "If truth be told
I must return. The lure of costly jewels
or other riches does not interest me.
I didn't leave one trusted slave or friend
to guard my goods. This journey across sea
for tidings of my father may well end
in my own death. An ambush lies ahead
set by those foul suitors who want me dead."

Now hearing this, the king without delay
went to his storeroom. Queen Helen joined him there
with their son Megapenthes. In this place lay
treasures of the royal court, fine and rare.
Menelaus chose a wine cup and his son
a silver mixing bowl to give their guest.
Queen Helen moved aside when this was done
to where rich woven clothes lay in a chest
and rooted there and then bent down to lift
a royal robe, bright with embroidery,
woven by her own hand, a perfect gift.
When this was done, they returned instantly,
crossing the great courtyard and stepping through
into the hall to meet the waiting two.

There King Menelaus, followed by his son,
placed their presents, glinting silvery,
before Telemachus. When this was done
the queen approached, so close the prince could see
each detail of her beauty. That flawless face
had launched a thousand ships, had brought Troy down.
"Hold this royal robe in a guarded place
known only to your mother. Give this gown
to your bride before you wedding day
and let her know it was a queen no less
who wove this gift. If she asks, you can say
it came from Helen, wife of Menelaus.
May the gods who rule our world accompany you
and grant you strength to do what you must do."

When the gifts had all been packed away
inside the chariot they sat to dine.
Choicest meat was served with a fragrant tray
of loaves freshly baked, and the finest wine.
But soon the two young princes rose to go
and strode outside. Their chariot stood there.
Now red-haired Menelaus, his movements slow,
stood by the tugging team and with due care
raised a golden wine cup in his right hand
so, his guests could make a drink offering.
"Farewell lads! When you reach old Nestor's land
[years ago, he took me under his wing
at Troy's great war] I charge you both to send
heartfelt wishes from an indebted friend."

Telemachus said. "Nestor will hear
your gracious words. Someday I hope to tell
my own father how I was welcomed here".
Just then, wheeling towards a nearby hill,
a mountain eagle flew overhead,
a white goose in its claws, this heavy prey
hooked from a farmyard. The bird veered, then sped
towards the chariot, then moved away
after it had circled it. This strange sight
caused so much wonder in the angry crowd
chasing from the farm, that they went quiet.
Nestor's son spoke first, calling out aloud
"This is a sign, sent by the gods on high.
Great king. What does this omen signify?"

While Menelaus paused, his mind searching out
an answer, Helen herself made reply.
"This omen is from the gods, have no doubt.
There's so much more to this than meets the eye.
Just as that mountain eagle swooped to kill
an unsuspecting home-fed goose in broad day,
so, Odysseus will soon return to spill
the lifeblood of these suitors; make them pay
for their arrogance and greed. I can see
the time of righteous vengeance has drawn near.
His days of wandering by land and sea
are in the past." "Your words have eased my fear"
Telemachus said. "May the gods bless
your life ahead with health and happiness."

He cracked the whip. The horses sped away
across the courtyard and soon were out of sight
through open countryside. All through the day
the two men rode. As dusk gave way to night
they stopped at Pherae for much needed rest.
At daybreak there they hitched the team once more
and journeyed onwards, always moving west
until they arrived at Pylos' sandy shore.
Telemachus turned to Nestor's son and said
"This bond of friendship forged between us two
feels watertight, to last the years ahead
and knowing that, I feel I can ask you
to do what I request. First hear me out
and you will help me then, I have no doubt."

"Lead me to my ship and leave me there,
for if you bring me to your father's hall,
his hospitality will be a snare
to hold me here. I must obey the call
from the god on high and sail home straightaway."
Peisistratus nodded "I will inform
my father as to why you could not stay.
Set sail at once for he will surely storm
his way down to the shore [I know him well!]
and insist you stay with him as his guest
if you're not out at sea by then. Farewell
my friend may your homecoming be blessed
with good fortune." They rode down to the sea
where the ship was moored, then parted company.

As the crew prepared to sail, suddenly
a man appeared at Telemachus' side
and said to him "I can clearly see
you are to sail out on the evening tide.
May I ask your name and your native place?"
"I'm from Ithaca." Telemachus said,
searching for my father, lost without trace
Odysseus is his name he may be dead
but I'll run the flag of hope up the mast
'till I know for certain that he is gone.
My name is Telemachus, an outcast
from my father's court but I'll leave no stone
unturned to banish those that forced me out.
I will be avenged in full; have no doubt."

"I'm Theoclymenus" the other said
"I killed a cousin in my own homeland
of Argos. Now his blood is on my head
and I have to leave there. You'll understand
my predicament, being an outcast too.
Take me on board, I'm seeking sanctuary."
Telemachus smiled "You may join my crew
as we sail to Ithaca. I will see
that you are treated as my personal guest."
He beckoned him aboard. They sailed away
and aided by a wind sent from the west
by Athena made swift progress that day.
That night they moved eastward, avoiding shore
as the goddess advised the night before.

Meanwhile Odysseus sat to eat that night
with the loyal swineherd. When they were done
he said, "Friend Eumaeus, it isn't right
that guests should overstay. I will be gone
at dawn to town, if someone guides my way
and beg for food and drink down at the port.
It's in my mind that later in the day
I might head to Odysseus' royal court
and tell my news directly to the queen.
Or I may join the suitors, volunteer
to be their servant. I can cook and clean,
bring their food to the table, serve wine or beer,
Daytime, nightime at their beck and call.
I'd work, no job too big, no job too small."

The swineherd cried "This is a foolish plan.
Those men are violent and won't treat you well.
Why would they take you on, an old, stooped man
when they have nimbler slaves to do their will?
You are more than welcome here and should stay
until Odysseus' son returns. I know
he will give you clothing and guide your way
if asked, to anywhere you wish to go."
"May Zeus reward you for your generous heart"
Odysseus said "I'll do what you have said
but I have questions for you now. I'll start
by asking are Odysseus' parents dead
or living still? They were both elderly
when he set off for Troy across the sea."

"His father is alive, advanced in years
but hungers every day for death instead"
Eumeus said "Laertes cries constant tears
for his long-lost son, sensing he is dead.
He also mourns his wife, taken from his side,
heartbroken when Odysseus left home.
She was a mother to me, a loving guide,
nursing me as if I were her own.
[her daughter and I were similar in age]
When the princess married, I had to go,
but was rewarded [better than a wage]
with this farm, with new clothing, head to toe.
Blocked by violent suitors there is no way
to meet queen Penelope. I have no say."

"Let me hear the story", Odysseus cried
"How as a child you were sold in slavery
to King Laertes." "My friend," Eumeus replied
"Those autumn nights are long, but company
mixed with strong wine will ease our journey through.
Sleeping too long is bad, the wise men say.
As for my farmhands, they have work to do
come morning and will have to slip away
for a well earned rest, leaving us two here,
I am content to do what you request.
Because my memory of that time is clear
and as host I should entertain my guest.
Sharing unhappy memories, I think
benefits the teller too. Let us drink!"

"Syrie was my home; my father was its king.
My story commences that fateful year
Phoenician sailors came ashore, trading
trinkets from a black boat moored at the pier.
Father had a Phoenician slave at court,
a lady beautiful in form and face.
This woman, washing clothing at the port
met, then fell in love at first embrace
with a trader on that ship. As they lay
in after-love, she shared her history
"I'm from Sidon, my father, locals say,
is the richest man in that territory.
Arubas is his name. A childhood blessed
with joy, a joy that fate was soon to test."

"One afternoon, while playing in a lane,
I was caught by pirates and sold in slavery
to the local ruler. Ktesios is his name."
The trader replied "Come away with me
on board our ship. We'll take you out of here
to Sidon, return you to your homeplace."
She agreed, but insisted, out of fear,
that all was done in secret just in case
the news of what was planned might reach the court.
She also insisted each sailor swore
that she'd be safe on board from leaving port
right through the voyage to her own home shore.
They all agreed. When this was done, the crew
made plans with her to see this venture through."

"Knowing she'd have to pay her passage out,
she promised that she'd steal some gold at court.
She also pledged [to leave them with no doubt
that she could pay] that she would bring to port
her master's little boy – she was his nurse.
They could use me as a slave, then trade
me at a further port for a rich purse.
For a year the Phoenicians stayed
and when the bartered cargo was on board
they sent a messenger to the palace
bringing a necklace with him from their hoard.
While my mother and her servants admired the piece,
he nodded to my nurse then slipped away.
His signal given; he ran back to the quay."

"When he had gone, the woman took my hand
and led me to the royal dining hall.
She snatched three golden goblets as she'd planned,
then hurried me so fast, I thought I'd fall,
through darkening lanes as the sun went down.
We reached the ship and joined the traders there.
With urgent strokes the oarsmen left the town
dwindling in their wake, out past the pier
to open sea. For six long days we sped,
wind in our sails, but on the seventh day
my nurse screamed suddenly and fell down dead.
They picked her body up from where she lay
and threw her overboard, right in my sight;
leaving me stunned, motionless with fright."

"We sailed on and by the following day
we came to Ithaca. Laertes bought me
as a slave. Now, my friend you know the way
I landed here, you know my history.
Your tale has roused my pity, that is true,
but Zeus, who heaped such sorrow on your head,
and you, so young, send good fortune too,
the gods can balance scales for men, it's said.
You had the luck to enter service here
with a master who treated you so well.
He left you with his farm from what I hear.
My life is worse than yours I can tell.
I'm spun out in roaming from shore to shore;
an exile all my days; my heart is sore."

Meanwhile Telemachus had made land
on Ithaca at a secluded bay.
His crew waded towards the sloping strand
in a wash of ripples. Later that day
he stood before his shipmates as they ate.
"Sail around the coastline to the port
while I move inland to check on my estate.
I'll meet you before long and will report
any news I hear, and when that's done
we will celebrate our safe voyage here."
Telemachus turned away and would have gone
but Theoclymenus said "I'm unclear
as to where I'm meant to stay. Do I go
to the royal court now? I need to know."

"My friend, I'm sure if things were otherwise
you'd be welcome to join my family.
But as things stand right now it would be wise
to give our court the widest berth. You see
I won't be there to treat you as my guest.
As for my mother, she stays in her room
while suitors downstairs carouse without rest.
She spends her time weaving at her loom.
There is one man among the rabble there
Eurymachus, the leader of that pack
who you might ask for lodgings if you dare.
He hopes to win my mother's hand, his track
to replacing Odysseus as her lord.
But Zeus on high may have the final word."

He'd barely spoken when a hawk flew by
[Apollo's messenger] holding a dove
and plucking it, so that feathers fell from high,
floating, as if directed from above
to land between the ship and where they stood.
Theoclymenus whispered in his friend's ear
"Such bird signs are omens – this one is good.
Your family will prevail, have no fear."
Telemachus smiled, called one of his crew
"Peiraios, I value your loyalty
on land and sea. Take home this man with you
and treat him as you would have treated me."
The crewman bowed "I swear this will be done.
He will be in my care, while you are gone."

When he had pledged this, Peiraios turned away,
wading through the breakers towards the ship,
followed by the crew. Without delay
the oarsmen took their seats and took firm grip
of their blades. Telemachus stepped on board
before the mooring ropes were all untied
to take his bronze pointed spear and his sword
from the deck. He watched them from the quay side
as they dipped their oars and pulled out from the pier
towards open sea, vanishing from view.
As he neared the swineherd's farm he could hear
the sound of grunting pigs. He strode right through
the gate. The fierce dogs, rising to attack
whined with joy now the young prince had come back.

Father and Son meet

Odysseus, sitting in the hut now heard
a crunch of footsteps on the pathway.
"Eumaeus" he called to the old swineherd
"Either a friend of yours is on the way
or a farmhand or some familiar face,
for all your fierce guard dogs have remained quiet."
As he spoke, his son entered the place.
The swineherd rose, exclaiming in delight
and kissed the young man's hands and eyes and head,
like a father greeting his long lost son.
"Telemachus, you have returned" he said
"Safe and sound from Pylos. Your travel's done!
For long years now, you've seldom called to me;
do you prefer the suitor's company?"

"I've called here first", Telemachus said,
"For news of my mother since I've been gone.
Did a suitor have his way – has she wed
after long years living all alone."
The swineherd gently smiled and then replied
"Your mother hopes Odysseus will appear
even though she's told that he has died."
Eumaeus reached and took the bronze edged spear
from the young man's hand. Odysseus stood
yielding his couch in honour of this guest
but Telemachus said, "It's right you should
remain where you are seated. Any chest
or makeshift seat of wood or straw or stone
will satisfy me better than a throne."

Odysseus sat. The swineherd made up a seat
from brushwood with a fleece for his young guest
then gave them wine, bread, and cuts of roasted meat.
When they had eaten, Telemachus pressed
his host with queries. "Tell me, who's your friend?
Where is his homeland? How did he come here?"
Eumaeus replied "Crete is his native land
but he was taken as a child from there,
spending most of his life in slavery.
He worked hard all his life; now comes my way,
a tired old man, to seek your sanctuary."
Telemachus spoke. "It grieves me to say
that what you ask of me I cannot do.
Let me explain my reasons to you two."

"Let me admit this. I myself am young
untrained in arms, unseasoned in the fight.
If I take you with me, we will be flung
among the wolves that prowl by day and night
through my home [those suitors wish me dead].
My mother's at wit's end and must decide
if she stays faithful to her lost lord's bed
or choose a suitor and so throw aside
my inheritance. Now, as for your friend,
I can give him food and clothes to wear
so, he's not a burden here or else send
him well armed, well shod and well dressed from here.
I am sorry. I cannot guarantee
his safety if he comes to court with me."

Hearing this, Odysseus addressed his son.
"Young prince, permit me to have my say.
When I hear what those upstarts have done
it grieves my heart. But why do you give way?
Are all the locals now your enemy,
stirred up by an oracle from the gods?
What of your brothers – it's right a family
should join together to improve the odds
when one of them is backed against a wall.
If I was Odysseus' son, I'd prefer
a suitor's sword to slice my head than fall
in with such a rabble, each one a cur.
Better a fighter's death than have to view
the ongoing misdeeds of this loutish crew."

"Overall, the people are on my side,"
Telemachus said, "but I'm an only son
with no brother to call on as a guide.
My station is a troubled, lonely one;
forced from my own house by a cutthroat crew,
with each one vying for my mother's hand,
while she holds on, not knowing what to do.
She has lost her husband, were I to stand
against the suitors she would also lose
her son – for they have vowed to murder me!
Eumaeus, go at once and bring the news
that I am here to Queen Penelope.
Take care, old friend, no servant overhears –
your words are only for my mother's ears."

Eumaeus nodded slowly then replied
"Surely Laertes should be told as well?
He has lost heart, convinced Odysseus died
years ago; sorrow seals him in a spell.
Since you sailed to Pylos he sits alone
in grief; food and drink untouched on tray.
Once sturdy, now the flesh falls from his bones."
The young man answered "Return straightaway
and let my mother send her housekeeper
to Laertes with news his grandson's back."
His urgent words acted like a spur
on Eumaeus who turned and left the shack
without a single word, without delay.
Father and son watched as he strode away.

Observing these proceedings in disguise
[this time as a lady elegant and tall],
Athena stood, unseen by mortal eyes,
but for those of Odysseus, along a wall
outside the gate. The guard dogs crawled away
from the goddess, whimpering in fear.
She gestured with her eyebrows: without delay
Odysseys crossed the yard to join her there.
"Son of Laertes! It's time for you to show
your son you have returned alive and well
to join him in his fight to overthrow
the suitors. If he's fearful, you can tell
that I, Athena, who's been your constant guide
will be there to fight with you at your side."

Athena touched him with her golden wand,
transforming him from grey-haired frailty
so that he stood, unwrinkled, lithe, and tanned.
This done, the goddess left immediately.
When Odysseus strode back and joined his son
Telemachus cried out in shock and fear.
"Old man, who can explain what has been done?
Are you a god? If so, why appear
before me in this place and in this way?
Perhaps I have upset the gods on high?
I will make sacrifice and hope to sway
their dreadful judgement, let them hear my cry
for mercy and forgive my foolishness."
He knelt before Odysseus in distress.

"Why take me for a god?" Odysseus said
"I'm your father who left his infant boy
so long ago that many say I'm dead."
With that he embraced his son; tears of joy
welled in his eyes and coursed along his face.
Telemachus, wide eyed with shock, went tense
and moved from this unexpected embrace.
"You are not my father! This makes no sense.
Why are the gods intent on tricking me
into thinking Odysseus has returned
home after all these years. Such sorcery
will not work on me for I have learned
that falsehood often wears a fond disguise:
everywhere I look, deception lies."

Odysseus answered swiftly "Oh my boy!
I am your father – absent since that day,
twenty years ago, when I left for Troy.
But I have come back home. I'm here to stay.
And now my son, as for my change of skin,
the great Athena fashioned that disguise
to hide me even from my kith and kin."
Half blinded by the tears that brimmed his eyes,
Telemachus embraced his father there
who also wept. The two men, chest to chest
cried like eagles whose shrieks tear through the air
when hunters rob their fledglings from the nest.
They clung together and cried helplessly:
from wells of longing drawing ecstasy.

They might have stayed like this all through the day
had not Telemachus asked suddenly.
"My dear father, tell me without delay,
what vessel carried you across the sea
and home to Ithaca? Who were your crew?"
Odysseus said "Phoenicians brought me here,
renowned sailors and friends of travellers too,
who give free passage to all calling there.
They set me down on Ithaca with gold
and bronze and gifts of woven cloth as well
[now hidden in a cave]. Athena told
me to travel here, then she cast a spell
transforming me completely, frame and face
so that I'd seem a stranger in this place."

"I need to know what faces me my son
how many suitors will we have to fight.
So, count and list them for me, one by one:
this knowledge will be helpful, will shed light
on our best approach, take them on alone
or else seek help." Telemachus cried
"The great warfaring deeds that you have done,
your skill in strategy can't be denied,
but it's madness to think that me and you
could take them on. Listen and I will tell!
From Dulichium there are fifty-two,
twenty from Zacynthus, twelve as well
from Ithaca, from Same, twenty-four.
For all I know of it, there may be more!"

Odysseus replied "Cast your fears aside.
Athena will help and Zeus, her father too."
"A mighty pair to have fighting on your side"
said Telemachus – "if what you say is true?"
'They will be there all right," Odysseus said,
"As we give those bastards a bloody end.
Now listen well. At daybreak go ahead
and join the suitors. Later I will wend
my own way there to check things out at court,
disguised as a beggar. If you should see
that those upstarts insult me just for sport,
if they rough me up or throw things at me,
rein in your temper. You might even plead
on my account; though they won't pay you heed."

"After that Athena will give the word
and I will nod my head – a sign for you
to round up every spear and shield and sword
left in the hall by that carousing crew.
Lock them in the weapon store upstairs.
If they ask you, be smooth in what you say.
Try this! "The soot and smoke from all these fires
has left them looking dusty, dull, and gray.
As well as that, I had a dream last night
where Zeus warned me to take them out from where
the suitors sit and drink in case a fight
leads to a young man's death by sword or spear.
That would invite bad luck for everyone;
leaving each man's courtship hopes undone.""

"Choose two swords and lances and hide them well
along with two shields – all for you and me.
Now one more thing – make sure you do not tell
a soul that I'm back – secrecy is key;
neither my father nor the swineherd here,
nor Penelope, nor her servants too.
We'll test the waters first so we can hear
who is false among the slaves and who is true."
His son replied. "I'll do everything you say,
but we'll waste time by checking everyone
while suitors feast by night and laze by day.
We could question the housemaids one by one
but leave the rest until the time is right,
until we know the gods will aid our fight."

Meanwhile Telemachus' vessel reached port
and there the gifts from Pylos were stored away.
A messenger was sent out to report
to Penelope her son had made his way
up country and was alive and well.
Now, as chance would have it, both this man
and the loyal swineherd, with news to tell
reached the court together. The first one ran
blurting out before the handmaids there.
"Your son's ashore today, take heart my queen"
The swineherd whispered in the queen's own ear
the message from her son and left, unseen
by the suitors who gathered all dismayed
as the crewman's message had been relayed.

They set up council then outside the gates.
Eurymachus spoke "The young pup's done it
and made it home! Our ambush party waits
to snare him but has missed the lucky shit.
Send word they should return immediately."
Just then Amphinomus, craning seaward
caught sight of their vessel on the sea.
He could see the crewmen at work on board,
reefing sails before each one took his oar
to bring the boat to land. "No need" he cried
"they're on their way and soon will be ashore."
Eurymachus nodded and then replied
"They must have seen the prince's ship slip past
and gave chase, but it must have been too fast."

At this they moved downhill towards the ship
to meet Antinous and his downcast crew.
"I can't believe he's given us the slip!"
cried Antinous "What more were we to do?
We posted scouts along the cliffs each day
and never slept ashore but when dark night
closed in, we went on board and there we'd stay
on sea watch until the rose-hued morning light.
We must not let him slip our net again
but must act carefully. The lad is young
but has proved to us he has a nimble brain.
Who knows that he may go and sit among
the assembly and try to stir them up
against us all? We need to stop this pup!"

Antinous continued "The people here
would send us into exile if they heard
we tried to kill him. To me, it's clear.
We need to act and put him to the sword
in some quiet place. Then we'll share his property,
stores and livestock among us straightaway.
When this is done, then we might agree
to let his mother and her new man stay
in the house. Otherwise, we let him live
and take his appointed inheritance.
If we choose that course, then we have to leave,
with each man returning to his own place
to court the Queen. But she may make us wait
sometime before she names her chosen mate."

Amphinomos, liked by Penelope
for his courtesy and his cheerfulness,
now broke the silence. "Friends, it seems to me
that we must ask the gods above to bless
this cold murder that we propose to do.
If Zeus approves, then I will undertake
to do the killing, with or without you,
but if the gods decide it's wrong to take
this young man's life then we must take heed
for men who go against the gods will pay
the price." The suitors, clustered round, agreed
to do as he advised, then made their way
inside the castle gates, out of the sun
and reached the dining hall, all talking done.

As they arrived indoors, Penelope
suddenly appeared before them all,
having been informed of their treachery
by Medon. He had heard them in the hall,
plotting her young son's death. The queen drew near,
scorn and anger flaring on her face
and spoke to Antinous without fear.
"Although it has been claimed around this place
that among your peers you are unsurpassed
in eloquence and in sound judgement too
that's not so! How long must this madness last?
Why are you still plotting among this crew
to end my dear son's life; turning deaf ears
to a mother's pleading, a mother's tears?"

"Those to whom great clemency has been shown
enrage Zeus if they ignore other's pleas
for mercy. I am sure you must have known
that your own father, pleading on his knees,
fled for protection to our family.
He joined Taphian raiders against our friends,
the Thesprotians. For this piracy
he would have met a rough and bloody end;
an angry mob outside, with knives in hand,
ready to cut the heart out of his chest,
slaughter his herds and commandeer his land.
But Odysseus made him welcome as a guest
and held them off. Despite this you carouse
without due respect in Odysseus' house!"

"To make it worse", Penelope went on,
"You woo his faithful wife against her will
and also plot to trap his only son,
who, for your plans to work, you have to kill.
I call on you to end this straightaway!"
Eurymachus answered Penelope,
"Lady! Shake off these ugly thoughts I pray,
and do not fear, for I will guarantee
to kill the man who dares to take a stand
against your son. As a child, I recall
the great Odysseus took me by the hand
to feed me from his own plate in the hall.
So, I'll protect your son as best I can;
though the gods alone decide the fates of man."

He spoke kind words, but all his words were lies.
Hearing him, Penelope made her way
to her rooms, where with heartfelt tears and sighs
she wept for her dear lord all through the day
'till Athena eased her with sleep at last.
Meanwhile Odysseus, his son at his side,
heard the swineherd's footsteps as he passed
the farmhouse gate. Both men moved outside
to hear the news. Unnoticed then, by the fair
Athena, with one movement of her wand
transformed Odysseus; figure, face and hair
back into ragged age so that he'd stand
disguised; for if the swineherd were to see
Odysseus he would tell Penelope.

"Welcome Eumaeus", Telemachus said
"Have the suitors all returned to base
or waiting in ambush for me instead?
Forgive me prince, but it was not my place
to find that out – I'd other work in hand;
though one of your men got ahead of me
and blurted out to all that you'd made land.
One thing I do know, with some certainty:
I saw a ship, with well armed crew on deck
sailing towards the pier as I left port
and assumed [though I did not stop to check]
it was the suitors." Making no retort,
Telemachus nodded, then taking care
Eumaeus could not see, smiled at his father there.

Odysseus returns to his own home

As dawn bloomed in the east with rosy light,
Telemachus, eager to make his way
to court, laced his rawhide sandals tight
and gripped his lance. "Friend, I must not delay"
he told the swineherd. "Unless my mother sees
me in the flesh she won't believe I'm here.
Take this poor man with you when you please
so, he can beg in town. I cannot spare
time to care for him." Great Odysseus said
"I'd prefer the town as all beggars do;
there's more chances of alms or wine or bread
where crowds dwell. Later, we will follow you
when the rising sun warms up my thin clothes,
for it's a long walk into town, I suppose?"

Telemachus left them, travelling downhill
at speed, nursing vengeance and planning doom
on the suitors; never stopping until
he reached the palace. In the dining room
he met old Eurycleia, covering chairs
with soft fleeced rugs. She stopped work instantly
and ran to him, her eyes welling with tears.
Other servants followed. Soon the hue and cry
reached Queen Penelope who hurried there
to hug her only son and kiss his face.
"You're safely home from Pylos! A mother's prayer
is answered. Against my will you left this place.
Since that night I have feared the very worst;
a husband and son both lost; doubly cursed!"

"Hold back your tears", Telemachus cried,
"Or else, because of all that I've been through,
I might cry as well. How I feel inside
must not be shown. Listen! What you must do
is leave this hall, head upstairs to your room.
When you have washed and dressed, then you should pray
the gods will help us plot the suitor's doom
and pledge due sacrifice. I'll make my way
to meet Peiraeus, who, at my request,
has taken a fugitive into his care.
I will bring this man home now as my guest."
Without a word, the queen made swift repair
to her room upstairs to bathe and to dress,
she then made offerings for Zeus to bless.

Telemachus strode outside, took his lance
and with two hounds at his heels left for port.
Athena sheened the young man with such grace
that crowds surged round him as he left the court;
among them suitors, primed with friendly words
despite their plot against his family.
Ignoring them, he made his way towards
old Mentor of well proven loyalty,
there with Antiphos and Halitherses too,
to tell them of his trips by sea and land.
As they conversed, the spearman of his crew,
Peiraeus, just as Telemachus planned,
approached, Theoclymenus with him there.
The young prince broke off talking to meet this pair.

"Send your servants to me", Peiraeus said,
"To bring the gifts of Menelaus back here".
"No mortal man can know what lies ahead"
the prince replied. "A suitor's sword or spear
may strike me down without a warning sign.
If that happens, you or another friend
should have those gifts. But if revenge is mine
and I drive these dogs to a bloody end
then bring the gifts to me without delay".
He brought Theoclymenus inside
and soon the two foot weary comrades lay
in polished baths. When they had been dried
and anointed, with fresh sandals on their feet
and with fresh clothes, they both sat down to eat.

Spinning wool yarn and sitting to the side,
the queen stayed still until the meal was done.
When they were finished, she looked up and cried
"I'm asking you the second time my son.
Before I retire to my lonely bed,
before the suitors swarm back to this hall,
is my long lost husband alive or dead?"
Her son replied "I will tell you all.
We went to Nestor's court – no news there
of father but Nestor sent his son with me
on to King Menelaus of the red hair.
I met Queen Helen there – for whose beauty
great Troy was toppled. Greeting queen and king
I explained the reason for my journeying."

When I told my story the king burst out
"These cowards want to creep their slimy path
into a hero's bed but have no doubt,
Odysseus will return in righteous wrath
to seal their fate. Once I saw him fight
brave king Philomelides of wrestling fame
and smash him down to the crowd's wild delight.
If he meets the suitors, he'll do the same;
swift death dealt out, no talk of wedding hopes.
I was told by the Ancient of the Sea
Odysseus is alive, but sits and mopes
on nymph Calypso's island sanctuary.
He has no ship, no crew, no sail, no oar
and pines; a lonely captive on her shore."

Her son's tale made the queen's heart stir with joy,
but Theoclymenus, if divining fame
now spoke. "O Queen, you've listened to your boy
but hear me out. I will call upon the name
of Zeus himself to witness my prophecy.
Odysseus has returned. He is at rest
or on the move, plotting a strategy
to bring black doom upon the vipers' nest.
Know this! I read that omen yesterday
at sea, told it to Telemachus too."
"Stranger" said the queen, "if what you say
is to be if this prophecy is true
then you will be welcomed here as a friend,
for bringing my long sadness to an end."

Meanwhile, in their high and mighty way
the suitors gathered in a level place
outside the palace as they did each day.
There they sported, either in relay race,
in javelin throw or discus rivalry.
As evening shadows lengthened on the track,
the herald Medon addressed the company
[he was friendly with all that boorish pack]
"Young men, it's time to come indoors", he said
"And make arrangements for our meal inside."
Hearing this, they left their contests to head
into the hall. They cast their cloaks aside
then slaughtered sheep and goats and pigs as well,
then sat down to eat in the timbered hall.

Meanwhile Odysseus prepared to leave for town
with the loyal swineherd at his side.
"You should stay here" said Eumeus with a frown,
"But my master ordered me to be your guide;
let's start our journey while it is still day."
Odysseus, who had it planned out in advance,
answered him "My friend – you lead the way.
Give me a stick to help this old man's balance:
I'm told that this path crosses hilly ground."
As he spoke, he slung his shabby knapsack
and then took the stick which the swineherd found.
They set out on the narrow mountain track.
Eumeus in front, completely unaware
that he had lord Odysseus in his care.

They set out then and later that evening
stopped at a well, its waters cold and clear.
The locals drew their water from this spring
and lay offerings to the nymphs. As they stood there
Melanthius, with two helpers at his heel
[they were driving young goats, chosen that day
to be killed for the suitors' evening meal]
approached the weary friends. "Out of our way!"
he snarled. "What a sickening pair to meet;
swineherd and pig [a stinking beggar too
who stands at doors, whining for scraps of meat!]
Give him to me – I'd find him work to do,
mucking out the pens or feeding the herd.
I'd make a farmland of him. Mark my word!"

"This man is a chancer, a layabout
who only wants to beg from day to day,
avoiding honest work. I have no doubt
that if this lazy rascal makes his way
to Lord Odysseus' hall he'll leave there sore
from flung footstools aimed at his head and back."
With that he kicked out, with a savage roar,
at Odysseus' hip to knock him off the track.
Odysseus kept his balance, wondering
if he should turn and beat him black and blue
with his stick or lift and hold him wriggling
then smash his head against the ground, but knew
he must hold his wrath for what lay ahead,
so made no response; did not turn his head.

It was the swineherd who stopped as he replied
"Melanthius – may Zeus heed my prayer
that Odysseus will cure you of your pride
and poor manners too." "You think I care?"
cried Melanthius. "Sometime very soon
I'll pack you on a slave ship overseas.
I hope Telemachus dies this afternoon,
killed by Apollo or cut down to his knees
by the suitors and let you know from me
Odysseys won't be coming home; he's dead,
killed on some foreign land or lost at sea".
Anxious to go, he turned and strode ahead
to join the suitors, [his friend among them all
was Eurymachus] feasting in the hall.

The two men followed on, eventually
reaching court. As harp music rippled through
the air, Odysseus cried "It seems to me
this must be Odysseus' place. I tell you
I never saw a palace so well set;
its stout walls guard this maze of buildings well.
I can hear the merry noise of banquet
from that spacious dining hall and can smell
meat on the spit." Smiling, Eumaeus said
"You are observant, but we must decide
if you join the suitors and beg for bread
as meals are served or if I go inside.
Don't delay too long if you chose to wait
or you'll be found and booted out the gate."

As full of guile as ever, Odysseus said
"You go in first and I will move around
the courtyard here. Don't fret! I've kept my head
through trials at sea and on the battleground.
Let new ones come; though hunger is a curse,
the cause of disputes, bitterness, and pain,
leading men to robbery [even worse!]"
Just then an old hound, lying in the drain
lifted up his muzzle, his ears pricked high
as Argos heard his master's voice once more.
He was Odysseus' puppy in days gone by,
now abandoned, full of fleas and sores.
For years the young men hunted hare and deer
with him, but now he lay discarded here.

Hearing his master's voice, the faithful hound
wagged his tail, nose down with flattened ears,
having no strength to move. Turning around
Odysseus raised a hand to hide the tears
wetting his cheeks from Eumaeus at his side.
"To leave a hound lie in this state is wrong,
he must have been a fine dog once" he sighed
Eumaeus said "The finest, quick and strong.
A hunter owned him when Odysseus went away;
no other dog could beat him to the scent.
But that man died abroad, and since that day
misery has him on leash, starved and spent."
Having seen his master, with one last breath
Argos closed his eyes into a dreamless death.

Eumeus crossed the square, went straight ahead
into the hall among the suitors there.
Telemachus, with a slight nod of his head
gestured to where there was an empty chair
beside him and they began to eat.
Soon afterwards, Odysseys came inside
his own doorway, shuffling on his feet
and settled on a wooden sill beside
the entrance. Taking meat and soft bread as well
Telemachus placed these on a tray.
"Bring this Eumeus to our friend and tell
him too when he's eaten to make his way
to beg for more among the diners here:
a beggar's need must rise above his fear."

The swineherd rose and moved back to the door,
"This tray of food is from the prince's hands"
he said "but he says that you must beg for more;
something that every beggar understands."
The great tactician lifted up his head
"May Zeus bless Telemachus" he replied
"I will do that". He took the meat and bread,
as beggars so, with palms held out then sighed
with pleasure as he placed the loaded tray
on his knapsack and ate each morsel there.
Meanwhile the court harpist began to play
and as sweet music rippled on the air
silence descended on that noisy hall
till he stilled his strings, let his fingers fall.

Unseen by all the revellers in the hall,
Athena stood at Lord Odysseus' side
and whispered in his ear "Go beg from all
the suitors here, swallowing your pride.
You might find who are decent, who are not
although not one of them will fly their fate."
With open palms he walked among the lot.
They gave him scraps, discussing as they ate
where he came from. Melánthios roared
"The swineherd brought this beggar here today;
I met the shabby stranger once before
as for the blackguard's name I could not say.
There's one thing that is absolutely clear;
it is the swineherd's fault that he is here!"

Antinous rounded on Eumaeus then
"Why did you lead this ragged rascal here,
this smelly pig you've released from your pen?
We've had enough of that sort, have no fear;
plate-licking tramps, the lowest of the low."
"You are a well born man" Eumaeus cried
"But that was not well said. The servants know
your harsh ways well – it cannot be denied
that you're the ringleader of this dogrough crew.
You treat me with especial cruelty
but still I know, despite the worst you do
that I have friends at court protecting me
with Queen Penelope a gentle friend
and her son to help me. My woes will end."

He broke off suddenly, catching the eyes
of Telemachus who now approached his friend.
"Eumeus, a word or two to the wise.
This man is dangerous and likes to bend
others to his will." He spoke in scorn
to Antinous himself. "This is my hall,
yet you dare to throw this stranger, lowly born
into the night. Before this crowd I call
on you to give this man some food to eat."
Antinous replied. "You are a fool,
he has enough!" Reaching at his feet
he held up as if to fling a foot stool
at Odysseys but suddenly turned back
as the others placed food in the stranger's sack.

Odysseus spoke "You seem to be well bred
and so should show a far more open hand
than the others here – choice cuts of bread
and tender meat so that in every land
I visit I'll praise your generosity.
I myself was wealthy years ago.
In my court it was never said of me
that I refused a beggar or was slow
to help a traveller in need of aid.
I had servants at my beck and call,
my ships were famed for plunder and for trade
in far off ports but my star was soon to fall.
Men satisfied with their life often find
that Zeus above has other plans in mind."

"I sailed to Egypt with a stalworth band
of sea rovers, our motives purely greed.
When we had berthed on the Nile's broad sand,
I placed guards on board, sent patrols at speed
to scout ahead, but they attacked a farm
killing what men, they found and took away
wives and children. Local towns took up arms
and by sunrise of the following day
we were surrounded by horse and infantry;
their scything weapons left our dead piled high.
A few were taken into slavery
including me [I'd have preferred to die]
Dementor, king of Cyprus, bought me there
but I've escaped his clutches and come here."

Antinous shrugged, replying with a sneer
"What evil wind blew in this noisy pest?
As for my friends you find so giving here
it's easy to be generous as a guest
with someone else's food!" Odysseus said
"You sit here fattened on other's meat, I see
and yet you grudge me one single crust of bread?
You wouldn't give a pinch of salt for free
to your house servants from you own food store"
Red faced with rage, Antinous let fly
the stool, meaning to leave Odysseus sore.
It might have been the impact of a fly
on Odysseus' muscled back who stood stock still,
and reined his temper in, through force of will.

Odysseys just walked past, shaking his head
then sat down at his door side sill again.
Facing the silent crowd, he smiled and said
"Blows that come through self defence in the main
can be accepted but this one was unfair.
Because I begged for food this man hit me.
If the gods take notice or if they care
for unfortunates like the one you see
in shabby clothes, then Antinous will pay
heavily for the wrong that he has done
in bloody death before his wedding day."
Antinous replied, his face as set as stone
"Enough of this, or we'll pull you by the heels
out of this court, until your back skin peels."

Out of the crowd, one of the suitors said
"A tramp could be a god disguised, to test
our mortal manners." Antinous stared ahead
without reply. Though utterly distressed
to see his father treated in this way,
Telemachus hid his thoughts from all there.
Meanwhile the queen had learned, to her dismay,
what had taken place. "It is my prayer"
she told her servants, "The god Apollo's bow
might strike Antinous and leave him dead.
If the gods allowed it, before the cock crow,
the others would also die," the queen's maid said
"Antinous is the worst among them all"
the queen cried, "striking a poor stranger in my hall!"

The queen called Eumeus "Without delay"
she said "bring that poor stranger here to me,
so that I can welcome him. He might relay
some scrap of news, some clue, some memory
of my lost lord from all his wandering."
"That man has been a wanderer for years",
Eumeus said. "The tales he told would bring
the gods above to wonder and to tears.
He's from Crete, claims Odysseus as a friend
from long ago. He says that he has heard
your husband is alive, and near at hand
in Thesprotia. He also gives his word
that Odysseus will soon be home once more,
his vessel laden with a treasure store."

"Let this stranger retell his tale to me
as the rest revel, draining our supply
of food and wine. They have it all for free.
Should this go on, our cellars will run dry,
our pantries and storerooms empty out.
No hero like Odysseus takes a stand
against these vultures here but have no doubt
if he came with his son at the right hand
these crimes would be avenged, he'd kill them all."
Just then they heard a most tremendous sneeze
from Telemachus in the dining hall.
"That is a sign the words I've spoken please
the gods! The suitors' end will come, it's clear.
Go quickly now and bring that stranger here!"

"Ensure that the stranger is made aware
that if he tells the truth of what he's seen
he will be given brand new clothes to wear."
The swineherd brought the news from the queen
to Odysseus who said "Tell her, I pray,
I will be more than happy to relate
all that I know, but ask her to delay
our meeting till tonight if she will wait.
Looking at the suitors in this court,
I fear their violent ways; not long ago
one of them, out of arrogance or sport
hit me on the shoulder – a coward's blow!
Neither yourself or Telemachus tried
to help me out, no one took my side."

The swineherd returned to the waiting queen
who met him at her threshold and cried out.
"Have you not brought him yet? What does it mean?
Is he afraid of something, or in doubt
that I'd listen to him with patient ears.
Shyness in a beggar is no good mark".
"He's no fool, Eumeus said, "for he fears
that suitors' offensive ways may well spark
into violence against him if they hear
that he's being singled out to meet with you.
He says it's best to wait 'till night is here,
more private for you as well." "That is true"
the queen replied. "He shows much sense, I see,
in what he plans and shows respect for me."

Eumeus returned to the hall at speed
and whispered into Telemachus' ear.
"Young prince. I must leave the court to feed
my pigs tonight. Your proper place is here.
I worry for your safety in this place
for there is danger lurking. Mark my words,
there are suitors here, who to your face
will smile but will wait with ready swords.
May the watching gods above destroy them all!"
He replied. "Take some meat and wine and bread
before you leave. At dawn, come to this hall
with beasts for slaughtering". When he had fed
on roasted meat and gulped a cup of wine,
Eumeus left the court to feed his swine.

The Beggar in the Palace

Just then a real tramp appeared at court,
renowned for sharp temper and gluttony,
all bluster and no balls. Just for sport
he was nicknamed Irus by the company.
This blackguard saw Odysseus at the door
and sensed a rival beggar in his place.
"Move from my spot or I'll leave you sore!"
Odysseus turned and stared him face to face.
"There's room for both of us to beg for food
but do not threaten me or I'll dye red
your lips and ribcage with your own blood,
leaving this begging place to me instead.
You'd never return to Odysseus' place
and none would miss your ugly, dirty face."

"Old man. I'll knock you sensless to the ground
without one tooth intact", the tramp replied
"I know you wouldn't last a single round!"
Overhearing this exchange, Antinous cried
out merrily. "My friends, this could be fun!
Our Irus and this stranger in the ring."
The suitors roared approval and everyone
crowded round the ragged pair. "One more thing",
Antinous called out. "Whoever wins this fight
can dine on stuffed goat's pudding – a real treat –
and beg from us at table every night;
the only beggar allowed in here to eat."
The others all agreed, then hurried out
into the evening air, to watch the bout.

Odysseus replied, quick thinking on his feet.
"There's no hope for an aging wreck like me
against a younger man but I need to eat.
To make things fair, I ask the company
to swear no one here will lay a hand
on me or help Irus in any way."
This was done. Before the watching band
Odysseus stripped his outer rags away
and practiced feints, performing for the fight,
showing his brawny thighs and arms and chest.
Those watching yelled in wonder at the sight.
"The muscles on that man! He'd be a test
for a fighter in his prime, without a doubt.
Irus will be hard pressed to win this bout."

Watching on, Irus shivered, cold with fright
but was dragged into the ring straightaway,
Antinous jeered at him "Afraid to fight
this old wreck? If he wins, then you will pay.
I'll ship you out to Epeiros. Its mad king
will slice your nose and ears with his own blade
and cut away your private parts and fling
them to his dogs." Now thoroughly afraid,
Irus advanced to meet his crouching foe.
Odysseus wondered what was his better course:
to send Irus to his death with just one blow,
or else to strike him with sufficient force
to knock him out? The second was the best
to avoid suspicion among the rest.

The two men circled one another now,
then Irus lunged, striking Odysseus near
his shoulder blade, but with a mighty blow
Odysseus' fist smashed under Irus' ear
breaking his jaw. A stream of bright red blood
ran bubbling from his mouth and he fell down,
heels drumming on the earth. The suitors stood
jeering as he lay screaming on the ground.
Then Odysseus hauled the fallen one outside
by the ankles and propped him at the gate
with a begging stick in his hand and cried
"Keep this for dogs and pigs; you're in no state
to take on other men for if you do
- take my word – something worse will happen you."

Odysseus returned to his begging place
and as the laughing suitors flocked inside
each greeted him with handshake and embrace.
"May Zeus and all the gods be on your side"
they said, "for ridding us of that foul pest."
Odysseus took this as a prophecy.
Antinous marched past and placed the best
pudding on a plate. Then, for all to see
Amphínomos added two loaves of bread
and brimmed a golden goblet with red wine.
"Your health, my ancient friend", he said,
"May your victory out there be a sign
that the gods are with you – good times are back!
Sit down and eat. Enjoy this tasty snack."

Odysseus answered him "From what I hear
your father was a decent man, whose word
was binding, without favour, without fear.
Your nature seems the same. Let me be heard;
take these words as advice and warning too.
No mortal knows what Zeus may send his way.
I found out to my cost that this is true.
I was successful once but went astray
and lived a lawless life. Behold me now!
You and your friends are living dangerously,
taking a great king's stores. You also show
his wife great disrespect. Listen to me!
Leave this place at once for the day is nigh
when the king returns and all of you will die."

Odysseus sipped the wine and bowed his head,
then placed the golden goblet in the hand
of the young man who, chilled with sudden dread,
turned back to sit among the revelling band.
Not that his fate could have been turned away,
for Athena had him well marked down to die
by Telemachus' hand. Later on, that day
Queen Penelope, not knowing why,
felt compelled to join the suitors as they dined.
She did not know this thought had been placed
by the goddess Athena in her mind.
Athena hoped that all the suitors faced
with her beauty would woo her all the more,
watched by her son and husband at the door.

Not knowing why, she had this urge, she cried
to her old, trusted nurse. "It's in my mind
to go among the suitors though I've tried
to keep my distance up to now. I'll find
when I've done this, an opportunity
to speak to Telemachus one to one,
advising him to shun this company;
their smiling faces mask danger to my son."
"Well said lady! But you must not depart
without bathing first and dressing in your best
even for your son's sake." "I have no heart
for such things. I've been careless how I've dressed
since my husband sailed away to Troy.
Such arts seem senseless now; they hold no joy."

"Inform my maids to come downstairs with me,
I should not face these men downstairs alone
all I have been left is my modesty."
When the nurse had gone, the queen sat on her throne
but Athena spun sleep across her eyes,
and as she slept, smoothed her tired face,
made her godlike, with golden arms and thighs.
When this was done, the goddess left the place.
The queen awoke and stroked her satin cheeks
"I wish the gods would let my death descend
as gentle as that sleep! Zeus knows I seek
this wretched, lonely life of mine should end
since my brave husband left me years ago
to days of misery, to nights of woe."

She rose and hurried to the dining hall,
two handmaids with her, one at either side.
The suitors saw her, elegant and tall,
with a veil across her cheeks to hide
the perfection of her face from their eyes.
In that instant, every suitor in that place
was flamed with lust and each, with longing sighs
wished to lie beside her. She turned her face
to her boy and whispered. "For shame, my son,
that you let a stranger to our court
be so abused! If through what was done
to this poor guest through cruelty or sport
left him injured then whose other name
would people call? You would get the blame."

Telemachus whispered, lips to her ear.
"I am all alone, lost among this crowd.
There was little I could do. Have no fear
the stranger has not been hurt, not even cowed.
The suitors hoped that Irus would defeat
the stranger in a boxing match today
but the visitor knocked him off his feet
with one strong blow. I can only pray
the mighty gods one day might let me see
these suitors beaten down like Irus here;
weak-kneed, punchdrunk and staring listlessly
at passersby who shake their heads and jeer
to see him slumped and broken at the gate.
May Zeus arrange that this will be their fate!"

Interrupting them Eurymachus cried
"If all in Argos had chance to see you here,
there would be hundreds more to crowd inside
this dining hall tomorrow. It is rare
that great beauty and wisdom so well combine."
"I've had no comfort from those qualities"
she answered him, "for all I do is pine.
My life is worthless, full of miseries
since Odysseus left. I recall that day,
he held me by the wrist and said to me.
The Trojans are great fighters too, men say.
If I am killed or held in slavery
[the gods decide the fate a man must face]
then you must rule Ithaca in my place."

"Take care of my parents as you have done
even more so," he said, "when I'm away,
and when a beard has darkened on our son
then marry whom you will. And so today,
now that Telemachus has come of age,
I must wed one of you – it breaks my heart!
But something else moves me to tears of rage,
that, as suitors, you do not play your part.
You should bring gifts as rivals for the hand
of a rich man's daughter and a queen as well!"
When he heard what Penelope now planned,
Odysseus was delighted. He could tell
she was charming gifts from everyone
with talk of marriage – though intending none.

Antinous replied, "Each man here is free
to make arrangements so gifts are carried here.
You must accept these out of courtesy
but we ourselves won't leave – I'll make this clear
until you choose one of us in this place."
They all approved, and each man sent a squire
to get the gifts: robes of exquisite lace;
rare jewellery – warm amber and cool sapphire,
necklaces, throatbands and fine earrings too
as well as brooches, chains and golden rings.
When these and other gifts were carried through
the door, Odysseus smiled to see these things
brought there by cleverness. The queen left court;
her maids carrying treasures of every sort.

The suitors continued feasting through the night
and soon large braziers were moved inside
the dining hall to give them warmth and light.
Stores of fuel – firewood, seasoned, split and dried,
were carried by house maids as flames sank low,
brought in wicker baskets to feed each fire.
Odysseus spoke to the maids. "You should go
to your queen upstairs to play the lyre
or else card wool to keep her company.
Don't worry about these fires. I'll stay here
to make sure they stay alight. You can trust me.
Even if they feast 'till dawn, have no fear,
I will not sleep on duty. So be gone
to your mistress who lies upstairs alone."

One of the maids answered, her manner bold.
This was Melantho, raised by Penelope,
doted on as if she was a royal child.
Yet this girl felt no love, no loyalty
to the queen, but boldly shared her bed
with Eurymachus. "You old fool", she cried
"Find a tavern bench to rest your drunken head.
Because you won a boxing match, your pride
has tricked you into thinking that your place
is in this court despite your looks and smell.
Some stronger man will fist you in the face
if you go on like this!" "Were I to tell
Telemachus", Odysseus cried, "You would pay
the highest price and lose your life today!"

They moved away, alarmed by his reply
leaving Odysseus to his duties there.
Athena now set words of mockery
in Eurymachus' mouth – she was aware
Odysseus' anger needed to be fed
like the fires he was tending through the night.
Seeking laughter from his friends the young man said
to the great Odysseus "Old man, tonight
I bring an offer of farm work to you,
planting trees for timber or clearing land
or building walls. You'd be fed and clothed too.
But I forget; you wouldn't lift a hand
for any honest work – it's not your way.
You only want to beg from day to day."

The great tactician smiled and then replied
"Were you and I to match ability
at scything grass, working side by side
through long summer days or else try me
at ploughing land with oxen well fed,
our two teams matched for pulling power and age
I'd furrow four straight strips of land ahead
of you! If great Zeus spurred me to engage
in war just now, I'd take a shield, two spears
and bronze helmet and you would see me there
in the front ranks. There would be no more jeers
about me! You think you are a great man here
among this craven crowd but have no doubt,
if Odysseus were to come back, you'd be out!"

Eurymachus, red with rage, made reply
"I will make you suffer for what you've said
before all my friends." Bending, he let fly
with a footstool aimed at Odysseus' head
but Odysseus ducked and the footstool clipped
a passing steward on his serving hand
so that his wine jug dropped, and the steward slipped
backwards and fell cursing to the ground.
With that, angry mutterings filled the air
as the suitors discussed the incident.
"Better if that beggar had died elsewhere
than coming here, ruining our merriment"
they grumbled, "and ruining our appetite:
this tramp has cast a shadow on our night."

Telemachus spoke "It seems to me quite clear
that you all had enough to drink tonight,
or else some god has goaded each man here
into petty rage, spoiling for a fight.
This is not an order, but I advise
it's time we finished here and took some rest."
Amphinomus answered "It is wise
to take sound counsel, so let no guest
harm this shabby tramp or indeed offend
any servants here. Now listen all,
let's raise and drink one final toast my friends,
then leave Telemachus in this hall
to take care of the tramp." When this was said
they drank, then reeled off noisily to bed.

The Telltale Scar

In that deserted hall Odysseus said
to his son "Take away all spears and swords
and lock them in an inner room instead.
If the suitors question this, use smooth words
to explain why their arms are stored away.
Tell them the blades are turning black in here
from smoky fires. If they persist, just say
you've moved them as it is your constant fear
they could be used in a drunken fight
drawing blood and shame on the company."
Telemachus nodded, while out of sight,
grey eyed Athena watched them quietly.
Then the young prince left the room to call
his loyal nurse and brought her to the hall.

"Nurse, make sure no servant can enter here
while I clear the dining room of swords and spears.
It's hard to keep the blades and handles clear
from smoke and soot that's built up over years.
I was a child when father sailed away
but now I am a man and want this done."
"It's time you showed an interest, I must say,
in this place as Odysseus' only son,
but who will guide you to the stores with light"
asked the nurse, "If housemaids are locked out?"
"The beggar here will be my help tonight"
he answered her. She bowed, then turned about
and went to lock the servants in their room;
leaving the two to start the suitors' doom.

They sprang to work when the nurse had gone;
father and son storing the weaponry.
Unseen by them grey eyed Athena shone
a lamp ahead of them so they could see.
Puzzled by the power of this light
Telemachus cried. "I've never seen
anything so powerfully bright."
"It's from the gods above; a sign they mean
to work beside us both," Odysseus said.
"I'll stay to put the queen's maids to the test
and your mother also. You go to bed
while I wait for her – you need to rest.
Tomorrow, we restore our family pride!"
Telemachus bowed, then left his father's side.

Penelope, beautiful and serene
appeared and sat down in her inlaid throne
made by Ikmálios and fashioned for the queen.
It had a footrest, over which was thrown
a heavy fleece. Two handmaids, at her side,
cleared the scattered wine bowls and crusts of bread
left by the crowd, lit fires that had died.
For the second time on Odysseus' head
the maid Melantho poured her scorn and ire.
"Still here? All you do is beg or leer
at maids. Get out, or with brands plucked from the fire
we'll scorch your arse and run you out of here!"
So, she raged at Odysseus as he stood
feeding the fire with handfuls of dry wood.

Odysseus glared at her and then he said
"Why attack a man when he's fallen low?
Every time I beg, my pride is shed
for I was wealthy once, I'll let you know
with many servants at my beck and call.
In my court, no beggar was turned away.
But Zeus, the great, ensured that I would fall
to poverty. Now heed these words I say:
You may soon find, unless you mend your ways
that your mistress may vent her rage on you.
Odysseus may return one of these days
and even if he's dead, his son will view
your bad-tempered tongue, your discourtesy
in the harshest light – just wait and see!"

The queen, being close enough to overhear,
spoke sharply to her maid. "You heard me say
I wished to question this poor stranger here
for news of my lost lord and you will pay
for deceiving me in Eurymachus' bed."
She called her housekeeper "Draw up a seat
and pad it with a sheepskin fleece" she said,
"So that the traveller and I can meet.
I'll hear him out, he may have news for me."
The chair and fleece were quickly put in place
leaving the stranger with Penelope.
She peered but did not recognise his face.
"Where have you come from friend? Who are you?
Your parent's names? May what you say be true."

"My gracious lady," the great tactician cried,
"For from this place, your name is rightly praised
among all people in towns or countryside.
Now as to these questions you have raised
about my origins, let me request
we speak of other things. My heart is low
from all the turmoils of my troubled past,
but if I weaken, let tears overflow
your maids [or yourself my queen] will think
that I have sampled too much wine tonight
and cannot control myself after drink."
The queen replied "I no longer take delight
in fame or looks. These things I've cast away
since my husband Odysseus sailed away."

"If my husband comes home again" she sighed
"My own good name might be restored to me.
Instead, I've been besieged on every side
by suitors who throng this court, making free
with our supplies. Each one makes his case
to marry me but I have not betrayed
my husband who no suitor could replace.
Worn out from all of this, I have not paid
due care to ruling Ithaca of late;
so much business that I should take in hand
is left undone. Meanwhile, I sit and wait
as young suitors press me, their passion fanned
by long delay. I've held them off for years
but now my day of reckoning appears."

"For three long years I kept them at bay
through trickery. I told them I must weave
a funeral shroud to be finished for the day
that Laertes, weak and old, would take his leave
of life. "You tell me Odysseus is dead"
I cried, "So that when I've woven this I'll choose
a husband from you all to share my bed."
They agreed, not knowing it was a ruse;
for by night, I undid the work of the day.
But a maid discovered what I had done
and let the suitors know without delay.
Now the shroud is finished, and I am undone.
My parents want me married and I hear
my son insists the suitors all leave here."

"But let me ask as I have asked before"
the queen continued, "of your family."
"Very well, although my heart is sore
recalling so much pain and misery.
There's an island kingdom; men call it Crete.
My father ruled this land and had two heirs.
Idómeneus, the older, joined the fleet
that sailed for Troy, was gone for ten long years.
I was the younger son Aithón by name.
Soon afterwards, Odysseus and his crew
were blown ashore [some god must be to blame]
at a nearby inlet. Odysseus knew
my brother – they were friendly, so he said
but he was gone, so I played host instead."

"So, I played host, my brother being away
lodged and fed Odysseus and his crew.
A storm blew up and raged for twelve long days,
so rough it was that all a man could do
was keep his feet on land – no chance at sea!
On the thirteenth day, the tempest fell
and they sailed away." Queen Penelope
sat and sobbed as she heard this beggar tell
of meeting with her husband years ago.
As she wept, the pale skin on her face
grew moist and glistened, the way that melting snow
spills down the hills and fills the streams to spate.
And so listening to his word, she cried,
little thinking her husband was at her side.

Odysseys looked at her as she cried
and ached to see his faithful wife upset.
He had the knack of keeping tears inside,
never blinking, as if his eyes were set
in ivory. The queen now spoke once more.
"Give me some proof, my friend, that this is true–
some details of the clothes my husband wore
at that time, and some details of the crew."
Odysseus nodded slowly, then he spoke
"It's twenty years ago but I would swear
Odysseus wore a thick fleeced purple cloak
held by a golden brooch, backed by a pair
of hollow tubes to hold its pins in place.
I'll tell you what was on the brooch's face."

"It was a scene depicted with great skill,
a hunting dog bringing a fawn to ground.
All done in gold – yet the moment of the kill,
the trapped deer looked so lifelike as did the hound.
Another memory has just dawned on me,
he wore a smooth shirt, gleaming like the sun.
I cannot say with any certainty
to you my gentle queen or to anyone
whether Odysseus when he sailed away
had those clothes or jewellery, or if a host
or shipmate had gifted them along the way.
I gave him gifts before he left our coast -
a lined tunic, a shirt and a bronze blade
in memory of a friendship, we had made."

"You also asked me of his shipmates there.
He kept one man at his side, I recall,
older than himself, with curly hair,
round of shoulder, dark complexion and tall.
He had a shrewd head like the captain's own.
Euybates was his name. Of all the crew,
Odysseus gave him preference." On her throne
hearing these details so minutely true
the queen sobbed once again and then she said
"Up to now you had won my sympathy,
but now you are my honoured guest instead.
I dressed him in those clothes when he left me
and pinned that golden brooch on that same day.
My heart was breaking as he sailed away."

"I realise that I will never see
my husband's face again or hold his hand"
the queen went on. "My life is misery"
Odysseus answered. "I can understand
how any wife would mourn the one she wed;
would grieve the man who lay with her in love
father of her children – and it is said
that Odysseus was like a god above
compared to other men. But dry your tears
I have some more news to tell, it is all true.
Your husband is alive after all these years
in Thesprotia and on his way to you.
He is amassing a fine treasure store
to bring to Ithaca; I'll tell you more."

"Your husband is alone. He lost his crew
who had slaughtered the cattle of the sun.
This angered great Zeus and the sun god too
who stirred a hurricane and drowned each one
but for Odysseus who was thrown ashore
in Phaeacia. The kindly people there
took him to their hearts, stowed a treasure store
on board a boat, gave him safe passage here.
He would have reached Ithaca long ago
but for his urge to travel far and wide,
gathering riches everywhere he'd go.
An urge so strong it cannot be denied.
Gentle queen, you can trust this news I bring;
I heard it in Thesprotia from the king."

"Phaidon, the Thesprótian king swore to me
that a ship lay rigged, seamen standing by
to bring Odysseus home. He let me see
your husband's treasure – it was piled so high
ten generations of his heirs or more
could live in wealth off that colossal hoard.
The man himself had left just days before
to Dodona to hear the sacred word
of Zeus from the oracle in the tree.
There he would find what plans to put in place
how best he might return home. Believe me
that this month, my lady, you will embrace
your husband and that day is coming soon:
between the waxing and waning of the moon."

"My friend, if what you tell me was proved true,"
the queen replied "my generosity
and friendship would make all men envy you;
but Odysseus will not return to me."
With that she turned to her maids and said
"Bathe our guest with oils and when this is done,
he will sleep tonight in comfort on a bed.
At breakfast, he will sit beside my son.
If any suitor tries to pick a fight
with this man, that suitor will not succeed
in any marriage claim. It is not right
that this poor stranger should remain in need
of bathing or of proper clothes to wear
at our table, while I am mistress here."

The queen went on. "Our lives on earth speed by.
Behind his back the cruel man is maligned,
then mocked in death but praise climbs far and high
for any man whose deeds and words are kind."
Odysseus answered, thinking on his feet
"My queen, I do not need a fancy bed.
I've had none since the day that I left Crete,
sleeping on hard earth or on deck instead.
As for bathing, none of these maids will do
to oil my feet, unless you have a maid,
old and wise who has suffered through
the years as I have done." Penelope said
"Dear guest. I admire your humility,
your tact and grace. What you request will be."

"I have a trusted handmaid, ripe with age,
who nursed my husband from his infancy.
She will tend to you, though at her stage
in life she is frail. Come out to me
Eurycleia and bathe this stranger's feet,
a man who seems the same age as my lord."
The old nurse moved Odysseus to a seat
and brought two water basins, hot and cold.
As she neared the man, Eurycleia cried.
"The gods above have been so hard on you,
wandering from your own home far and wide,
mocked by housemaids. Perhaps Odysseus too
is now being jeered at in some other place
by servants there, laughing in his face?"

"Whatever my queen commands I will do.
She said you are a stranger but to me
my lost master sounds and looks like you."
"Old woman – I'm sure many might agree"
he replied in a tone deliberately light.
And so, the old nurse, without any more delay
filled up the bath, glittering in firelight.
Now Odysseus abruptly turned away
from the fire so that he faced the dark,
remembering the scar that marked his thigh,
worried she'd recognise the telltale mark.
But when she bared his leg, she let a cry
seeing the familiar scar, she could not hide
a cry that was half joy, half terrified.

Following Odysseus' birth within days
his grandfather, Autolycus, arrived
[a rascal and a swindler in his ways]
to name the boy. "You know that I have lived
 at odds with men from countries far and wide"
he said "so call him Odysseus, son of woe.
Let him visit me in the countryside
at Parnassus when he grows up." And so
when Odysseus' beard first shadowed on his face
he travelled there, feasting that day and night.
In the morning the young man took his place
among the men to scale Parnassus' height.
They climbed till noon, Odysseus at the fore
behind the dogs, hunting the white-tusked boar.

Before them, a full-grown boar had its lair,
behind a thicket, sheltered from the wind
and hidden from sun. It had been sleeping there
but now awoke to the advancing sound
of men's feet, dogs' feet, barks, excited cries.
It charged out of its den and stood at bay,
sharp tusked with bristling back and flaming eyes,
facing Odysseus still leading the way
ahead of the rest, holding his long spear.
The boar attacked, gashing the young man's thigh
with its white tusk, leaving a jagged tear.
At the same time Odysseus arched, let fly
the bronze tipped spear. Unerringly it sped
straight through the creature's heart. The boar lay dead.

The other hunters, running up the hill,
found the lifeless boar and Odysseus in pain.
They stanched the blood and bandaged him with skill,
then brought him down the mountainside again.
He stayed with Antolycus to heal and rest
and then sailed back to his own family
with gifts from his grandfather in a chest.
This was the scar, just above the knee,
the old nurse saw. Abruptly she let go
her master's leg, causing it to drop
against the basin, letting water flow
across the floor. Her tears now fell non stop
and she whispered, her hands soft on his brow
"Odysseus it is you! You are home now."

She turned aside to tell the grieving queen
the news, but all her efforts came to naught
because Athena, waiting there, unseen,
had distracted her. Odysseus turned and caught
his old nurse by the throat with his right hand,
his left hand pulled her close and, in her ear,
he hissed "Listen to me and understand.
No one else must know that I am here
in Ithaca after twenty years away
to put false maids and suitors to the test.
You nursed me as a child, would you betray
the one that you suckled at your breast?
Take this as warning – and I mean it too;
keep your mouth shut tight or I will kill you."

The old nurse kept her wits and she replied
"You know I will stay silent as a stone
about your plans and I will take your side.
I'll tell you of the housemaids, one by one,
those who are disloyal, those innocent.
"No need" he said "I will check them all
so, hold your peace", those worrying words were meant.
In silence then, the nurse walked from the hall
and refilled the basin upturned on the floor.
After she had washed and oiled his feet
Odysseus moved and joined his wife once more
where she sat brooding in her fire side seat,
pulling his rags to cover up his thigh,
fearful that the scar would catch her eye.

The queen saw him approaching and she said
"It's time to go where others savour rest,
but as for me, when all the world's in bed,
I lie alone, heart thudding in my chest,
wondering if I should stay here with my son;
a grieving wife, though mistress of this land,
in loyalty to my husband, or else choose one
of these suitors who compete for my hand.
Up to now, I had my duties here,
rearing Telemachus on my own,
but now he has grown up, and makes it clear
that I should leave this palace my own home
naming a husband and a wedding date
before the suitors squander his estate."

"Another thing! I had a dream last night
about a flock of geese that feed on grain
not far from here – indeed it is my delight
to watch them. Now, in my dream, to my pain
a mountain eagle swooped, killed all the flock.
Some well-dressed ladies of the court came by,
to comfort me. And then - another shock!
The eagle returned, hurtling through the sky
then broke into human speech. "Have no fear,
this is no dream, but real as day," he said.
"The geese you see are suitors, it is clear
and I, not eagle, but your lord instead
returning home to clear these upstarts out
from my court in Ithaca. Have no doubt."

"Just at this point I woke and looked outside,
where in the yard my geese were safe and sound
pecking grains." Odysseus now replied
"The meaning of your dream is easily found;
Odysseus is giving you a prophecy
that the suitors will meet a bloody end."
"Most dreams are baseless", smiled Penelope,
"cobwebs of no significance, my friend.
Dreams with something to import are rare.
Because of that mortals must heed such dreams
as meanings the gods may want to share.
But as I think about it now, it seems
my dream last night was just a fantasy
with no hopeful sign for my son and me."

"But there is one more thing I wish to say,
the hateful day is drawing ever near
when I will leave this place, be torn away
from my husband's court which I hold dear.
I will declare a test of archery
involving twelve bronze axe heads and a bow.
My husband performed this feat frequently,
lining up the axe heads in a row,
then stepping back a long way off he'd send
an arrow through their rings – straight through them all!
The suitor who can manage this, my friend
will marry me. That day I'll leave this hall,
the place of many happy memories
for a new home in this land or overseas."

"Let this contest take place without delay",
Odysseus said "Your husband will be back
before any suitor here can find a way
to string Odysseus' bow and try that trick"
"We could talk all night" Penelope said,
"But mortals, unlike the gods, require sleep.
I will go upstairs to my lonely bed
where, like so many nights before, I'll weep
for my absent husband and curse once more
that city that stole him away from me.
You can choose to bed down on this floor
or on a soft guest bed." So, Penelope
went to her room, lay there with tears and sighs
still Athena cast sweet sleep upon her eyes.

The Trap is Set

When she was gone, Odysseus made a bed
from hides and fleeces, piled on level ground
beside the entry way, then laid his head
facing the moonlit yard. Without a sound,
Eurynome approached him as he lay
and gently placed a rug to cover him.
Sleep was slow in coming, his mind at play,
exploring in advance each stratagem
for the suitors' doom. Now as he lay there
a strut of maids, all giggling in delight,
slipped from the hall and moved across the square
to join the suitors in their beds that night,
as they had done on many nights before;
ignoring the man watching from the floor.

Anger surged in Odysseus at this sight.
What should he do? He was torn between
leaving these maids enjoy one last hot night
with the suitors [dishonouring their queen]
or else rise up and kill each woman there.
His heart growled with anger in much the way
a bitch will growl when danger comes too near
her helpless pups. But then he turned away,
muttering to himself. "This will take patience,
like when that great brute Cyclops ate my crew
as I looked on in shock. I had the sense
escaping would take time and much guile too"
And so Odysseus kept his rage on leash
and watched the women moving out of reach.

And still he lay, restless in his bed,
twisting and turning, rolling left and right
just like a cook, impatient to be fed
rolls a sausage on the pan. How could he fight
so many suitors here – what could be done?
From the night sky, to stand beside him there
Athena came. "O most unhappy one"
she said "You are sleepless, all racked with care,
although you're back in Ithaca again;
your true wife safely in her sleep upstairs
and your son here too. Can you explain?"
"That much is true, but I have two more cares"
Odysseus said. "The first is strategy
how can one man fight against an army?"

"My second worry now", Odysseus said
"if I kill these suitors where can I hide
to escape vengeance falling on my head?
Tell me that!" Grey eyed Athena replied
"Most met when faced by danger will seek aid
from other mortals but you rely on me,
a goddess. There's no need to be afraid.
You will succeed through guile and bravery.
So sleep my friend, for mortals need their rest,
all night vigils drain energy away."
With that the goddess moved her hands and pressed
soft sleep upon his eyes, then straightaway
lifted into the night, right off the ground
and was soon out of sight, Olympus bound.

Just as Odysseus settled into sleep,
his wife upstairs in bed, suddenly awoke,
and recalling her cares, began to weep.
When she had her fill of tears she spoke
in prayer to Artemis, "Let your bow
send an arrow through me so I might meet
my husband in the underworld below
for without him I am incomplete.
Let our lonely shades join in Tartarus!
I had a dream as I dozed in bed,
so real it shocked me into wakefulness
that Odysseus lay with me, head to head;
restored to youth, in vigour and in face
just as he was before he left this place."

Just then dawn lit up the eastern sky
and Odysseus, waking, could hear the sound
of his lady weeping. In his mind's eye
he approached her and as she turned around
she saw it was him standing by her side.
Then smiles replaced the tear drops on her face.
He shook his head then moved his bed inside,
clearing rugs and fleeces from the entrance
on to a bench, then raised his arms in prayer
"O Father Zeus! Send two signs to me;
one from the other world and one from here.
I have returned home, over land and sea
despite the many perils sent my way.
Show me now, you stand by me, I pray."

In Olympus. above the reach of cloud,
Zeus, without delay answered his prayer
and sent a peal of thunder, long and loud,
down to the palace, pulsing through the air.
The second wished for sign came to his ears
from a maid, grinding flour, all alone.
Twelve servants shared this job, but all her peers
were resting in their beds, their work being done
ahead of her, for she was frail and old.
She stopped, hearing the thunder's mighty boom.
"Lord Zeus above. Such thunder we are told
is a portent of impending doom
for those whose punishment is overdue.
Hear me now, make what I ask come true."

"Perhaps the gods above will pay some heed
to a tired old woman's beseeching call.
Let this be the last day these suitors feed,
filling their bellies in Odysseus' hall.
They work me to the bone, supplying bread
at every meal throughout each day and night.
May they feast no more", the maidservant said.
Odysseus heard her prayer with great delight.
This was the second sign from Zeus he knew
after the thunder that had been sent his way
out of the clear dawn sky, out of the blue!
Smiling to himself he turned away,
sensing that his revenge was very near.
He felt refreshed, renewed, released from fear.

Telemachus woke at the start of the day
and soon was dressed and armed with sword and spear.
Reaching the doorway sill, he made his way
to Eurycleia who was standing near.
"Was a bed prepared last night for our guest
or food and drink to sate his appetite?
My mother sometimes overlooks the best
and wastes her time with riff raff all the night."
"He had enough to eat" the old nurse said
"But for a bed he stretched out on the ground
under hides and fleeces. Under his head
I placed a rug and gently wrapped it round
the visitor as it was getting chill,
though when I left him, he was restless still".

Telemachus, spear in hand, moved outside,
his two frisky hunting dogs to his rear,
to the meeting place, fringed on either side
by pillars – the suitors were gathered there.
Eurycleia called the maids. "There's work to do!
Sweep the rooms; sponge the tables 'till they shine;
wash out the wine bowls and the wine cups too
and tell the cellar man to bring the wine.
Let others fetch fresh water from the well –
No loitering – come back here straightaway!
The suitors will come early to the hall
this morning as it is a holiday.
When you are finished, report back to me.
No time to waste, start immediately!"

The maids dispersed, twenty to the spring,
the rest went indoors to their various chores.
Other servants came to chop dry kindling,
splitting logs as fuel for all the fires.
Eumaeus, the loyal swineherd now came by
with three fatted hogs for the feast that night.
Seeing Odysseus, he joined him instantly
"My friend! I hope that you're being treated right
by the suitors?" Odysseus smiled and said
"These young wastrels have no spark of shame.
It is my hope that in the time ahead
the gods will let them wish they never came
to Ithaca. It is my constant prayer
that these bastards are driven out of here."

As they talked Melanthius drew near
[the goats herd who had insulted them before]
Seeing Odyssues, he said with a sneer
"You, again! Begging at a palace door.
If I had time, I'd beat you black and blue."
Odysseus glared but said nothing in response.
The herdsman Philoítios saw them too
and joined the swineherd at the entrance.
"Your friend looks down at heel, and yet he stands
beside you with the bearing of a king.
These gods control our lives; we're in their hands
like hooked helpless fish, twitching on a string.
None of us can escape what lies in wait;
prince or pauper none escapes his fate."

He then shook Odysseus by the hand.
"My friend! I wish you better days ahead.
When I saw you now, it struck my mind
that Lord Odysseus, if he isn't dead,
might be a ragged wanderer like you
in some friendless place. It's been long years,
and if what the suitors say is true
he is dead. If that is so, my tears
will flow, for he trusted me to care
for all his herd when I was just a lad.
These herds are countless now, beyond compare
throughout this wide world, but it makes me sad
that I am forced to slaughter cows each day
to feed these men who seem they're here to stay."

"These young men show no courtesy or fear
of the gods alone or Queen Penelope.
The only things that these rough men hold dear
are Odysseus' goods and his property.
I can't make up my mind what's best to do.
Should I desert this prince and go away
from Ithaca and work in pastures new?
Is it better to go or should I stay
here as I am, at the beck and call
of upstarts? I'd be gone long ago
to another king, to serve another hall
but I keep thinking [how I wish it so!]
that my dear master might return once more
and drive these ruffians out his palace door."

Knowing he would need allies at his side
Odysseus answered. "After meeting you,
I sense you are no fool and will not hide
from action but would see the fighting through.
So, listen to me now – this is no lie
[let Zeus be witness to what I have to say]
Odysseus will return home. So, stand by
and wait here 'till he makes these suitors pay."
"I hope that this is true", the man replied
"For if it does, I'll gladly volunteer
to join with him and fight there at his side
I'd show that I am handy with a spear!"
Eumeus echoed these words in his turn,
praying that his master would return.

Meanwhile the suitors gathered round to plot
Telemachus' murder. Suddenly above
an eagle swooped across the very spot
where they were standing, with a helpless dove
gripped firmly in its claws. "This is a sign
not to kill him here." Amphínomos cried
"Let us enjoy this holiday, with wine
and food and song." And so, they trooped inside
where each one threw his cloak across a chair.
Then the ritual slaughtering began
[sheep, goats, pigs and grass-fed cows all killed there.]
Then the entrails were roasted on a pan,
all served with finest wine and fresh soft loaves
by the swineherd, cowherd and Melanthius.

Telemachus placed his father at the rear
where he could observe the full company
and placed a battered stool and table there.
"Sit down my friend" he shouted "I will see
that no cutting comment, no cuffing hand
will upset a guest in my father's hall."
Turning round then, his face grim with command
he cried "That is a warning to you all!"
The suitors, taken by surprise, were quiet
though Antinous managed to have his say
"My friends, let's pay no heed to him tonight.
Great Zeus above has forced us to delay
or we'd have shut his mouth long before."
Telemachus shrugged but said no more.

And so, they dined on tender roasted meat.
Odysseus, at his son's direct command,
was given an equal share of food to eat.
All was well at first then one of the band
Ctesippus from Samé, rich and proud
[a fancied bidder for Penelope]
stood up at his table and cried aloud.
"Our begging friend is treated well I see,
so let me add my own bit to his share."
With that his hand went backwards and let fly
a cow's foot at lightning speed through the air
at Odysseus' head. Without blinking an eye,
Odysseus moved his head softly aside
so, the cow's foot hit the wall at his side.

Odysseus smiled grimly – his one response.
Telemachus blazed up "You were most lucky there
that you missed him or else I'd run my lance
through your heart! There would be no wedding here
but your own grave to break your father's heart.
As for the rest of you, let me not see
more of this behaviour. For my own part,
although I cannot fight a company
all on my own, I will not tolerate
any further discourtesy, you've said
you'll kill me soon. If that's to be my fate
that's good enough. It's better to be dead
than to see my father's house upset:
maid servants defiled and guests under threat."

Under his lashing tongue, they all went quiet
'till Agelaus spoke to the assembly.
"My friends. Telemachus is surely right!
We must treat this stranger with courtesy.
But let me say a word, both to the queen
and her only son. Year after year
you let hope root and blossom, tall and green,
for Odysseus' safe return. By now it's clear
he's dead. Penelope should choose a mate,
the richest or the best among us all.
Telemachus then won't have to wait
for his inheritance but can stand tall
as king of Ithaca, a fresh new start,
with the queen as mistress of another court."

Keeping his head, Telemachus said
"I will swear by Zeus and by the suffering
of my own father, who is either dead
or is lost, no more to rule as king,
that I will not place an impediment
to my mother. "Marry whom you wish" I say
and I will make a generous settlement.
But saying that, she won't be forced away
from her family home against her will."
Athena now confused the suitor's ears
so that they broke out laughing, loud and shrill.
But soon their braying laughter turned to tears
heart sore with a sense of impending doom;
seeing blood on every foodstuff in the room.

Theoclymenus, the prophet, now stood
and cried aloud "Doom gathers in this place!
These walls and furniture reek with blood.
I see the mark of death on every face
and lines of restless shades make their way
through these doors to throng the yard outside
on their way to the underworld. Today
foul mist surrounds us here; the sun has died."
The suitors laughed again and with a sneer
Eurymachus answered "His mind is gone.
Let's throw him out – he finds it too dark here
so let him see the sun!" "Leave me alone"
the prophet said. "I foresee that death will call
to all of you misusing a great man's hall."

The suitors rolled their eyes when he strode out
then made fun of Telemachus too.
"Strange guests you have invited here no doubt;
a beggar who, when faced with work to do
will disappear; and now this laughingstock.
Take our advice, my friend, and throw this pair
on a slave ship that's leaving on the dock
for Sicily – you'd earn some money there!"
Telemachus ignored the suitors' jeers,
watching his father for a sign to move.
The suitors' laughter reached the queen's own ears
as she watched from a hidden nook above.
Little did they know as they drank and ate
this would be their last meal: death sat in wait.

The Test of the Bow

Athena spun a thought in the queen's mind;
to bring the axes and Odysseus' bow.
These would start out as a taste of skills, then end
as instruments of bloody death. And so
the queen, bronze key in hand, slipped away
to the room where her husband's store of gold,
bronze and iron were kept – a rich display.
A sturdy hook was hammered high to hold
the massive bow, with arrows in a case.
Odysseus used this bow to hunt the hills
of Ithaca but left it in this place
vowing not to use it again until
he returned from Troy to his family.
The queen stood at the door and turned the key.

The lock moved sideways as she turned the key
and to her ears the inward swinging door
sounded like a bull bellowing angrily.
This was followed by light footsteps on the floor
as she moved inside. All round her there
lay chests of herb scented robes and a trove
of fine treasures assembled with great care.
But the queen's milk white arms reached above
all these and lifted from its varnished case
the mighty bow. Then sinking to her knees
she sobbed aloud, tears coursing down her face.
Then back she went to face the revelries
having called her servants to help her bring
Odysseus' weapons down to the gathering.

The queen, holding the unstringed bow in hand,
with a loaded sheaf on her back, now faced
the crowded watching hall. At her command,
her servants carried baskets which they placed
along the floor. Each one held an axehead.
There, in her beauty, she stood silently,
a shining veil across her cheeks, and said
"You have abused my hospitality
and persuaded me my lord will not return,
with each one competing to take his place.
So, here's my test for each of you in turn.
It's not a wrestling match, it's not a race
by foot or horse, it's not a discus throw.
I will explain the contest to you now."

"This is my lord Odysseus' hunting bow.
Bend and string it if you are able to
then let an arrow fly straight through a row
of twelve axehead sockets. I promise you
the one who can display the strength and art
that is required will have me as a bride
and I will leave my home, make a fresh start
somewhere else, a new husband at my side."
She said to Eumeus "Take these away
and place them in the dining hall on chairs."
The faithful swineherd sobbed as he made his way
with his master's bow in hand down the stairs,
and the cowherd too turned aside to cry
seeing Odysseus' treasured weaponry.

Antinoos glared at both of them and said
"Do you want to cause the queen more woe,
already grieving her husband who is dead?
Be quiet or go outside! Leave us the bow.
This test I see won't be an easy one.
Is there one man among our company
to rival Odysseys' strength anyone
to match his peerless skills in archery?"
He said all this, hoping those in the room
world be deterred from taking on the test.
But little did he know that his own doom
was already set as he would be the first
to die among that rough and rowdy band;
an arrow through his throat from Odysseus' hand.

Telemachus rose to his feet and said
"My dear mother at last has changed her mind,
now she's been convinced her husband's dead.
She seems content to leave this court behind
with her new lord. But now it's up to you
to show which man among you is the best.
She is a prize beyond compare, it's true.
Now first of all, I'll attempt the test;
and should I succeed with my father's bow
the one and only prize that I will win
is my pride restored, softening the blow
of parting from my mother. I will begin
my days as master here with inner joy
rivalling my father's feat - no more a boy!"

Telemachus leapt up from his seat
leaving his crimson cloak and sword aside.
And now he set himself to try the feat,
digging a trench with a ridge of earth beside
to line the planted axeheads in a row,
stamping the earth to hold them into place.
The suitors watched, stood wondering at this show
of workmanship. He now moved to embrace
Odysseus' massive bow with hands outstretched
to string it first, then try the challenge shot.
Three times he tried and failed, but as he stretched
the bow the fourth time, the string drew near its slot.
Just then Odysseys gestured with his head
so, his son lay the weapon down instead.

"Damn it! I seem to have no strength at all.
Let my elders and betters try instead."
He placed the unstrung weapon by a wall
and sat down again. Antinoos said
"Let's do this from left to right, one by one
from the corner there where they store the wine."
They all agreed that this should now be done.
Leódés, a seer, was first in line.
He hated all the rowdy arrogance
of the rest and sat apart at the side.
Approaching the great bow, he took his stance
but couldn't bend it, no matter how he tried
for he was puny, and his arms were weak.
He dropped the weapon and began to speak.

"I couldn't do this – let the next man try
this is a contest that will break the heart
and spirit of many in this company.
Let each man follow me and play his part
in this trial, but the chances are so low
that you'll succeed. You'll have to look elsewhere
for a bride." With a shrug, he placed the bow
against the door, returning to his chair.
Now Antinoos replied, flushed with rage.
"It is a contest that will break the will
and spirit of many...? Weak language!
You were too puny, with no strength or skill
to string or shoot that bow. But just take heed;
there's better men than you that will succeed."

He turned to Melanthuis, the goatherd
"Let's try a little trick that I know.
Kindle a fire and bring a cake of lard
from the stores to heat and grease the bow."
This was done and many suitors tried
but each one failed. Only two held back;
Eurymachus, with Antinoos at his side
[this pair were the leaders of the pack].
Two men separated from the rest,
the swineherd and the cowherd, both downcast.
Odysseus joined them, asking as a test
"If Odysseus came back home at last,
out of the blue as I myself have done.
would you fight alongside him and his son?"

The cowherd answered him without delay
"If Zeus would let him come, then you would see
I'd be no slouch or coward in the fray.
Eumeus also pledged his loyalty.
Hearing his faithful friends, Odysseus said
"I am Odysseus, returned home at last
after twenty years. Men presume me dead.
You are the only men that I can trust
along with Telemachus, my own son.
If you join with us, by Zeus I'd pledge
fatted swine and prime cattle for each one.
Should you wish, I'd set you up in marriage,
with houses built near mine for both of you.
Rest assured that all I say is true."

"But let me show a sign that I am he."
With that, lifting his rags, he bared his thigh
and showed the long boar gash. Instantly
they knew; no more needed to satisfy
themselves that their old master was really here.
They cried and kissed him; he embraced the two,
then cut it short and said [he had fear
that they would be heard by one of the crew]
"The suitors will try to overrule my call
to test the bow. Now Eumeus, at this stage
take the weapon and bring it through the hall
to where I am, despite their shouts of rage.
When we finish here, we'll go separately
inside, one of you in turn behind me."

"There's one more thing before our meeting's through.
The housemaids must be told to lock the doors
leading to their quarters – make sure they do.
If they should hear wild screams and groans and roars
of bitter fighting, none must show her face.
You, Philoetius, lock the gate outside
and slide its heavy cross bar into place."
With that he turned away and strode inside
then took the battered stool he had before.
They followed him, as agreed, one by one,
each man entering by a separate door
in the hall, unnoticed by anyone.
Odysseus sat quietly now at the rear
knowing the time to act was drawing near.

Meanwhile Eurymachus picked up the bow.
He turned round before the licking flame
to warm it up but could not, even so,
succeed where other men had failed. In shame
he muttered "How I wish I'd never tried
to join the rest of you at this hard test.
It's not so much the losing of a bride
[women are plentiful]. What hurts me most
is to be seen to be a boy compared
to Odysseus. I cannot even bend
his bow. There is no doubt I won't be spared
ridicule – to be repeated without end.
This shame I feel is surely shared by all
our comrades who are gathered in this hall."

"Control yourself!" Antinoos replied.
"I'll tell you now, we'll solve this problem yet.
Today's a holiday – let's leave aside
this challenge. Trust me, there's no need to sweat
over a bow! Let's leave the axes here
lodged safely in the earth for the night.
Time for food and wine to restore our cheer,
and when rosy dawn floods all the world with light
we will seek help, with all due offerings
from great Apollo, god of archery.
Then we'll try the bow and whoever strings
and makes the shot will claim Penelope."
They agreed to this; all sat down to eat
and drink; fine wine and joints of tender meat.

Odysseus addressed them, speaking with great care
"Good advice Antinoos, to leave the test
for one more day when you have offered prayer
to Apollo. But first may I suggest
you let me try my hand at this huge bow
to see if there's any strength left in me
after years of hardship – I don't think so!"
His request enraged all of the company
with Antinoos the first one to respond.
"It's not enough that we have let you dine
with us – a prize no other vagabond
has been allowed. You've gulped back too much wine.
Don't touch that bow! I warn you, don't compete
with younger men. Stay silent. Keep your seat."

The watchful queen Penelope replied
"This is not the way we treat a guest!
Are you afraid? Even if he tried,
and by luck or skill got through this test
you don't imagine that I'd go away
and join him in his restless, wandering life?"
Eurymachus answered her "We do not say
you would agree to be a poor tramp's wife
but should this beggar do what we could not,
the news would spread. "Those suitors could not string
Odysseus' bow or make the needle shot
and yet this wretch, worn down by travelling
comes out of nowhere and succeeds." My name,
the names of all men here, would sink to shame."

"Far too late to worry about your name.
You have abused a prince's court for years
feasting on his wine and food to your shame.
Give the man the bow now and if your fears
that he'll succeed at this are proved true.
I will gift him sandals for his feet,
a shirt and cloak, a lance and broadsword too
with passage to his home for his feat."
Telemachus strode up to her and cried;
being worried for his mother's safety,
"As lord of Ithaca I will decide
on this. Go to your room immediately."
She went to her room and there began to weep
for her lord 'till Athena sent her to sleep.

Now the swineherd took the bow in hand
moving towards Odysseus at the door.
Observing this, the suitors' anger fanned
from low mutterings into uproar.
"Where are you taking that? Return it now
or you'll end up as food for pigs to eat!"
He faltered, numbed by fear, set down the bow,
But prince Telemachus rose to his feet.
"Give him the bow! You take commands from me.
If Zeus would heed my call, I'd fling this crew
like dead rats through these palace gates." His plea
stirred laughter in one man which rippled through
the crowded hall. Unnoticed in the din
Eumeus lifted up the bow again.

Eumeus placed the bow in Odysseus' hands
who called his old nurse over to his side.
"Lock the women's door – my son commands.
Lock it tightly. If anyone inside
should hear screams and groans coming from this hall
she must stay put." The old nurse moved away
to lock the door unnoticed by them all.
Philoetius too, quietly made his way
catlike, running to bold the courtyard gate
binding it with deck rope and then returned
into the dining hall, prepared to wait
until the sign was given. He had turned
his seat so that he would, throughout the night,
have Odysseus directly in his sight.

Odysseus took his time, turning his bow
carefully, tapping either end to test
for termites. The suitors were all watching now
and mocked his every move with taunt and jest.
"Look at our tramp – an expert at all things!"
Great Odysseus ignored their mockery.
Like a harper, stretching a sweet new string
upon a peg, so then, effortlessly,
with one smooth motion practiced over years
he strung the bow, then slid his right hand down
the string and plucked it. To the listening ears
of the suitors and servants gathered round
the tautened gut vibrated – a sound as clear
as a swallow makes when danger is near.

Hearing that sweet vibration of the string
the whole hall hushed. Just then overhead
Zeus let one massive peal of thunder ring
above the roof. Odysseus raised his head
and smiled. He picked one arrow from the rest
then notched it in the bridge, snugly in place,
drew back the string and arrow for the test.
Still sitting on his stool, he turned to face
towards the target. From the twanging bow
the arrow flashed, cutting through the air,
through every axe head ring, twelve in a row,
not touching one hoop as it journeyed there.
The room stayed deathly still, no suitor broke
the silence but at last Odysseus spoke.

Bloodbath in the Great Hall

"Young prince Telemachus," Odysseus cried
"The guest that you have welcomed to your court
has not disgraced you here. You took my side
and let me chance my luck at this strange sport.
My hands and eyes are sound you will agree
despite what some others here have said,
but now they might not make such fun of me.
This crowd has come here to be wined and fed
on tender meat and finest wine tonight
and after that music, and dancing too."
He gave a nod, looking to the right
where Telemachus sat. Without ado
Odysseus' son, armed with spear and sword,
rose to his feet, waiting for the word.

Odysseus also stood and faced them all,
his bow in hand and arrow at his side
"I'll try another target in this hall,"
he announced. "May Apollo be my guide."
He notched an arrow then, and on it sped
towards Antinoos, sitting on his seat,
just at the moment the young man bent his head,
lifting a wine cup to his lips – that sweet
bouquet of rich red wine his final scent.
Odysseus' arrow struck below his chin
pressing up the feathers as it went
right through his throat, slitting the tender skin.
Antinoos fell backward then, the curled grip
of his hand released, letting the wine bowl slip.

Antinoos slid slowly from his seat,
his nose and mouth and throat all spurting red.
One last convulsive movement of his feet
knocked his table, scattering meat and bread
beside his lifeless body on the ground.
There was uproar in the hall, each suitor there
searched round for arms – not one lance could be found.
"You'll die for this and slowly too! We'll tear
you limb from limb. You've killed the very best
nobleman in Ithaca," they cried.
Little did they know, how could they have guessed
it was no accident their friend had died
but the first act of a stern, remorseless fate?
How could they know, their own death lay in wait?

Odysseus answered them with cold contempt.
"You dogs! You never thought I'd make it here
from Troy. In my absence you were content
to fleece my household without shame or fear.
You raped my maids and bid for my dear wife
while I was still alive. Your death is due."
Each man stood stunned, then fearful for his life
looked for a hiding place. One of the crew,
Eurymachus found strength to speak. He said
"If you are lord Odysseus home again
we have wronged you without doubt, but were led
by Antinoos, the one that you have slain.
He would have killed your son to become king
of Ithaca – power was the thing."

"Spare the rest of us and we will make
restitution for all the meat and wine
we have consumed and every loaf and cake.
Each suitor here will pay an honour fine
of twenty oxen, gold and bronze gifts too.
This way we can wipe our wrongdoing clear."
Odysseus glared "No treasure will undo
what you have done. There will be killings here
until that score is paid, have no doubt.
You have a choice, either stand and fight
or run for it – let's see you make it out!"
The suitors were ashen faced, numb with fright
but Eurymachus faced them in the hall
and issued one final rallying call.

"Friends," he cried "This man wants to kill us all
but he's alone. Let's fight him then, I say.
Draw your swords. Use the tables in the hall
to deflect his arrows. I'll lead the way
as we rush him – we're many against one!
We'll drive him from the door. When we get by
we'll seek extra help. His race will soon be run."
He raised his sword, let out a savage cry.
Before he could rise up to his feet,
Odysseus aimed and an arrow sped
right through his liver. He fell from his seat
scattering his wine bowl, meat and bread.
In his death throes, his head slammed off the floor
as both legs jerked. Then he moved no more.

Amphínomos, broadsword in his hand,
now raced forward, but Telemachus threw
his bronze edged lance and hit him from behind
between the shoulders. The force pushed it through
to his chest. Telemachus moved aside
around the fallen suitor, leaving the lance
planted in the dead man, for if he tried
to yank it out there was every chance
as he bent down, he'd be killed there and then.
So, he sped to his father at the door
"You are one against so many men
I will bring you weapons from the store
and arm our two comrades who will stand tight
alongside the two of us as we fight."

"Go quickly then and I will hold them here
while I have arrows left." Without ado
his son raced to the storeroom like a deer,
grabbing four light shields, eight lances too
and four plumed helmets. Rushing to the hall
he armed the others and himself – All three
stood with Odysseus, four backs to the wall.
His father had used his skill at archery
with effect, killing suitors one by one.
He fired a final shot from his great bow
as they armed and then, as they had done
armed himself, for he knew his crouching foe
could see that he had used his full supply
of arrows and would attack by and by.

Now there was a side door along the wall
from which a passage led to the store
where weapons had been moved from the hall.
Odysseus told Eumeus to guard this door,
just as a suitor Ageláos, cried out.
"If one of us could exit through that way,
we could alarm the town; I have no doubt."
Melánthious said. "One man could hold sway
against us all in that narrow space.
But listen! I will scale the wall instead
and bring arms from the storeroom to this place."
They all agreed, and so, with agile tread
he moved aside, then climbed and did not stop
'till, footsure as a cat, he reached the top.

When he had scaled the wall, he made his way
to the storeroom, then returned to the hall
and back three more times without delay,
taking shields and spears and helmets at each haul;
twelve of each, which he handed to his friends.
Seeing this Odysseus felt a rush of fear
inside him then said to his son "All depends
on the suitors being unarmed but now it's clear
we may lost this fight. Find out for me
who gave them access to the weapon vault
- it could be one of the serving maids maybe."
His son replied, "Father this was my fault
I left the door wide open to my shame.
It's all my fault; there's no one else to blame."

"Eumeus," he continued "lock that door
then check to see who took those weapons out.
One of the maids, familiar with the store
or Melanthius – a clever one, no doubt."
At that moment the swineherd turned aside
and saw Melanthius in the passageway,
heading to the storehouse. Eumeus cried
"Melanthius is the one! I'll make him pay
but tell me first which way it should be done?"
"We'll stall the suitors here," Odysseus said
"Let you and Philoítios now run
and tie him up – I do not want him dead
just yet. Lash him to a plank, – raise it high
and leave him there. We'll have him by and by."

When they reached the room, through the corridor,
Melanthius was there, his head bent down,
rummaging for arms. They hid by the door,
one on either side and made no sound.
When he turned round, hands filled with weaponry
they sprang and knocked him down and held him tight.
Then they tied him by hand and foot and knee
and hoisted him up to rafter height.
Eumeus jeered at him "Sleep well up there
throughout the night safe in your airy bed
until it's dawn when you will remain here
instead of driving prime goats to be fed
to your friends downstairs." They locked the door
leaving him in his sling, bruised and sore.

They rejoined the other two in the hall
and stood together, four against two score.
Out of nowhere then, standing by the wall,
Athena appeared as she had before
in disguise as Mentor. Odysseus cried
"Mentor, my old friend! Join us in our fight
[he sensed it was Athena at his side]
Agaláos called out. "You will die tonight
if you join with Odysseus and his son,
but a slit throat won't be the only price
that you will pay, for when the fighting's done
rest assured that you will be punished twice.
We'll take your home and all your property,
turning out your wife and family."

Now Athena, enraged at this low threat
turned on Odysseus "Where's your courage gone?
Great warrior at Troy, do not forget
that because of you and you alone
that great city fell. Yet here you stand
uncertain in defence of your own door.
Stand with me and we'll get the upper hand!"
Despite these words, Athena did no more
for the present, putting father and son
to the test to prove their bravery.
She vanished then; her rallying done
knowing he would respond to her plea.
Again, she changed her shape, unseen by eyes
a swallow on the roof beam; her new disguise.

Ageláos, who by now was in command
called his men together. "This is our chance!
Mentor has deserted him. Let's stand
in lines of six so each man throws his lance
at Odysseus along with the other five.
If we can kill the leader then have no fear,
his three friends won't come out of here alive."
At his command each one threw his spear
but Athena caused their aim to stray,
hitting doorposts, walls and doors instead.
Taking heart, the four, without delay
let fly their spears, leaving four suitors dead.
As they fell down, Odysseus and the three
rushed forward then to pull their lances free.

The suitors rallied but their spear throws missed,
for Athena spoiled their shots except for two
one grazed Telemachus on his wrist
one scratched Eumeus' shoulder then passed through
to clatter off a wall. And now the four
attacked again, killing with each throw
the last one Ctesippus, who, not long before
threw a cow's foot, hoping to make a show
of Odysseus. He liked to hurt or jeer
those he thought were weaker with his cruel wit.
Dying now, he heard those words in his ear
as Philotios hissed "You little shit!
This is payment for your discourtesy
to a great man, his wife and family."

More suitors died, falling one by one:
Agaláos struck by Odysseus' hand
sank to his knees and Odysseus' son
ran his spear at Leókritos from behind
right through his body, kidney through to chest
that he fell, head thumping off the ground.
Just then Athena's shield with her great crest
shook above them with a deafening sound.
The suitors, like cattle in mad stampede
running from a darting swarm of gad flies
turned and fled. With Odysseus in the lead
the attackers followed with savage cries,
like falcons swooping through the sky to kill
their prey with ruthless and relentless skill.

The pounced on their prey, weapons dripping red,
turning to strike with lunging sword and spear.
Each severed throat and limb, each hacked-off head
seemed to spur them on. The screams of fear
did not pause their merciless butchery
as men fell on the glistening, blood soaked floor.
Leódes fell down at Odysseus' knee.
"Spare my life. I have done nothing more
than read the signs, have done no wrong by word
or deed and often tried to stop the rest."
Odysseus frowned and reached out for a sword
"You read the signs for them, you were their priest
and prayed to bed my wife, so die you must."
He struck; the suitor's head rolled in the dust.

One other man approached him cautiously.
This was Phemios, the suitor's unwilling bard.
Before this he placed his harp carefully
on a seat, then stepped forward, clinging hard
to Odysseus' knee. "Your son will tell,
I never ate nor drank with this vile crew.
You will regret it later if you kill
a minstrel. If you save me, I'll sing for you
as I would entertain the gods above."
Now Telemachus, hearing this, called out
"Wait! This one is innocent. Do not move
against him! If you do, I have no doubt
that we will have to pay a heavy price:
far much more than normal sacrifice."

Odysseus nodded and let the minstrel free.
Now prince Telemachus again called out
"Let herald Medon live – he guided me
through my boyhood." Telemachus' shout
was heard by Medon underneath a seat,
hiding in utter fear, wrapped in a hide.
Throwing this off, he fell at the prince's feet.
"Speak for me lad, for I stood by your side
when Odysseus was away. Tell him so!
Hearing this Odysseus smiled and said
"You have no need to fear, you're free to go.
Stay outside this hall. More blood will be shed
but you are safe, yours will not be spilled.
Neither you or the minstrel will be killed."

The two men bowed and moved across the floor
around the bodies heaped up on every side.
They were nervous as they neared the door
fearing Odysseus might suddenly decide
to change his mind and kill them both instead.
Odysseus checked round looking left and right
for wounded men to kill but all seemed dead.
They lay in heaps like captured fish pressed tight
in fine mesh nets then spilled out on the sand.
And still he checked through that great hall of death
but saw no blink of eye or twitch of hand
no suitor stirred or made a single breath.
Satisfied at last, he called his son
"Find the old nurse. There's more work to be done."

Before long old nurse Eurycleia stood
facing Odysseys in the corpse heaped hall.
His face and limbs and torso shone with blood
and blood glistened on floor, on every wall.
Seeing all the dead men she raised her head
to give a cry of triumph but he said
"There's no honour in jeering at the dead,
the price of their wrongdoing has been paid.
Now this is where you must play your part.
Tell me who is guilty and who is true
among the fifty handmaids in this court."
"Twelve deceived the queen, deceived me too"
answered the nurse "often in open sight.
Will I inform the queen of this tonight?"

"Do not wake her yet. She needs her rest.
But bring the guilty housemaids here to me.
I do not want my wife to be distressed
by the sight of all this butchery,"
he exclaimed. He now turned to his son
and two comrades "Let's move the dead from here
with the women's help and when that is done
they can sponge the marks of bloodshed and clear
off walls and floor and all stained furniture.
When the hall is clean, take these maids away
and hack them with your swords until you're sure
not one is left alive. They too must pay
for what they've done. Tonight, each one lies dead
the price for lying in a suitor's bed."

As he spoke, the maidservants now drew near,
wailing to see their lovers lying dead.
Under command, they set to work to clear
the bodies to the yard, each maid in dread
of Odysseus who checked the work being done.
When they'd scrubbed the hall and rinsed the place
the swineherd, cowherd and Odysseus' son
forced them outside at point of sword and lance.
The women huddled, sobbing bitterly.
"You don't deserve a clean death," the young prince cried
"for deceiving my mother and mocking me!"
He found a mooring rope and this he tied
between two tall pillars, pulled taut and high.
The maids shrieked, seeing how they were to die.

They dragged each serving maid, then slipped a noose
into place, ignoring each scream and prayer.
Each woman struggled but it was no use
and soon all twelve of them were hanging there.
For a while their feet twitched but then no more.
Next, they brought Melanthios to the yard
from where they'd tied him in the weapon store.
They surrounded him, each one drew a sword
and grimly set about their work again.
At first his nose and ears were sliced away.
Then heedless of his helpless shrieks of pain
they hacked his prick and balls without delay
before they stopped; their butchery complete
by chopping off the goatherd's hands and feet.

They went indoors, their bloody work complete
and Odysseus called the nurse. "Bring sulphur here
to banish evil from this place. Then heat
the water bowls whose cleansing fumes will clear
this charnel room. Then tell Penelope
when you have brought the servants to this place."
The nurse replied. "It's wrong that they should see
you dressed in beggar's rags. You should replace
these tattered clothes." Odysseus shook his head
"The first thing we must do is purify
this court, where so much blood has been shed.
There will be time for fresh clothes by and by,
when all is done, and it should be done at speed.
Go quickly, bring back everything we need."

Penelope: The Test of the Bed

With no more chat, the old nurse left the hall
and brought back sulphur for the ceremonies,
then set the fires blazing along the wall.
Odysseus, after praying on his knees
went through the hall and yard and storeroom too,
according to the rite, with cleansing fumes.
Eurycleia, as she was asked to do,
now hurried away to the women's rooms.
Flocking from their quarters in torch light
they reached the great hall, impatient to meet
their lord. Each one wept tears of pure delight
and bent to kiss his hands and face and feet.
They lined up patiently, one by one:
in tears he stood there, naming everyone.

Old Eurycleia hurried up the stairs
urgent with her news, to the queen's bedroom.
"Odysseus has returned after these long years"
she cried "and the suitors have met their doom
at the hands of your husband and your son."
"The gods have touched your mind and maddened you"
the queen replied, "and now my sleep's undone!"
The nurse persisted. "What I say is true.
He returned as a beggar in disguise.
Your son has known of this some days ago
but did not tell the secret. That was wise,
allowing time for him to overthrow
these upstarts with his father and two friends.
Your husband has returned. Your sorrow ends."

The queen hugged her servant but then she said
"I cannot understand! If this is true
how come so many suitors could be dead
at the hands of so very, very few?"
"I did not see how this miracle was done
but heard groans of dying men in the hall"
the nurse replied. "Soon after that your son
sent for me [the house servants one and all.
were locked out of the hall some time before].
I found Odysseus standing all alone,
with corpses this way, that way on the floor.
He has cleansed the court with sulphur to atone
for the lives taken in this killing spree
and waits on you downstairs, impatiently."

"Come with me now, your husband waits downstairs
after long, lonely years of misery.
He is back home – an answer to your prayers!
He has dealt out death to those who made free
of his house." Queen Penelope replied
"Though what you claim would be a wish come true
the only reason that these suitors died
is through some god's anger, long overdue.
They have paid most dearly for what they've done
but my poor husband is dead long ago."
"How can you say this? He is with your son
downstairs and that is all you need to know.
You are mistrustful but now hear me out.
What I have to tell you will clear your doubt."

"I washed the stranger's feet [as well you know]
last night and noticed, halfway on his thigh
a scar – the very one caused years ago
by a mountain boar on Parnassus high
when Odysseus was gored while hunting there.
I would have told you but this he knew,
for he gripped my throat and hissed in my ear
that he would kill me if I informed you.
All this is true. I swear it on my life!"
"Nurse dear" the queen replied and shook her head.
"Though you are wise and shrewd, sharp as a knife.
The gods have you fooled, for my lord is dead,
But let us join my son. We may find out
how this slaughter of the suitors came about."

The queen went downstairs wondering what to do.
Should she question the stranger as a test
or, taking her nurse's story as being true,
kiss his hand and hold him to her breast?
Entering the hall, she chose the opposite side
to the bloody, ragged man and found a chair.
Observing him, she could not yet decide
if it was her lost lord sitting there.
Her son approached her, all stern faced, and said
"Mother – is this blindness or cruelty
that you sit apart from him you thought was dead?"
"I am stunned, my child," said Penelope
"but if it is he, I can soon find out
through private signs which will remove all doubt."

Overhearing this Odysseus smiled and said
"Telemachus, let your mother test
me at her will. The way I look has led
her to believe I'm just a tramp. It's best
to wait until she sees that I am he.
As for this massacre, we must take care,
for we have killed the aristocracy
of Ithaca, not in open warfare
but in a clever trap. Their families
will rise against us soon. What will we do?"
His son replied "Whatever strategies
you choose, myself and the other two
will carry out, with all our strength and skill.
We've stood alongside you and always will."

Shrewd Odysseus thought quickly, then replied
"Pretend to hold a wedding feast in here
so that no townsmen passing by outside
will think of killings. It will appear
one of the suitors has won my lady's heart.
This plan will give us time to slip away
to our farm. Now let the revels start!
Bathe, then dress yourselves in fresh array;
tell the servants to wear their finery.
Let our harper play dancing tunes all through."
This was done. The sounds of gaiety
was heard by those outside. "Who ever knew
our queen would wed again," they said. A shame
she couldn't hold on 'till Odysseus came."

Now Odysseus was bathed, oiled and dressed
by Eurycleia. Athena cast a spell,
lending him beauty, filling out his chest
and limbs, curling his gold-red hair as well.
He sat across from his quiet wife and cried
"Strange woman! The gods have hardened your heart.
What other wife would sit and turn aside
when her lord appears from whom she's been apart
for twenty years? Nurse – make me a bed!"
"Strange man – if man you are" replied the queen.
But nurse, let you do what our guest has said:
Place the bed outside my room and pile clean
thick fleece, then sheets and rugs soft and deep.
After his mighty deeds he deserves sounds sleep."

Odysseus turned on her angrily.
"Woman! Who has dared to move our bed?
No builder has skill for that – could it be
it was a god who managed this instead?
The bed was our secret – my work alone.
I built our bedroom round the sturdy base
of an olive tree, lined up walls of stone,
and roofed it watertight, then set in place
a solid double door. As a bedpost there
I used the smoothed trunk then made three more
all placed and inlaid with the greatest care,
using silver gold, ivory on all four.
I stretched a bed on oxhide straps between
the post – a fitting bed for king and queen."

"I know no more. Now you explain to me.
Has someone sawn that trunk to move our bed?
Eyes brimming with glad tears, Penelope
threw her arms around her husband and said.
"Forgive me. I've been deceived down the years,
by suitors and imposters who come here;
my heart turned wary and hard. Now my fears
are swept aside tonight by what I hear.
Three people know our secret- that's us two
and faithful Aktoris, my chamber maid.
My love is back! I can start anew.
It is for this that I have wept and prayed
to the gods above every night and day
those twenty joyless years you were away."

Now rising from his joyous heart, sweet tears
welled in Odysseus' eyes. He held her tight.
A moment, longed for over lonely years
as a shipwrecked sailor with land in sight
having survived when his ship went down
crawls through the surf, caked with brine, on to shore,
knowing he is no longer doomed to drown
out on high sea, safe on dry land once more.
And she, in turn, would not let him go.
At last releasing her, Odysseus said
"There's one more trial that I must undergo.
Tiresias warned in the land of the dead;
but first we need to lie down and to rest
in out secret bed- now I've passed the test."

Still clasping him his smiling wife now said
"We'll rest in bed together, have no fear
but tell me first of that trial that lies ahead."
"It's a dull tale but one you deserve to hear.
Tiresias told me to take an oar
and then wander round the countryside,
till I meet men who never saw before
the salt blue sea, the surge and race of tide,
or crafts with dipping oars like wings spread out.
There I'll meet a native who will say
"That's a spade or winnowing fan, no doubt
you carry on your shoulder." Straightaway
I must lower my oar and plant it there,
offering Poseidon sacrifice and prayer."

"After these sacrificial ceremonies
I must return to Ithaca once more
and offer burnt offerings to appease
all the gods this time. Tiresias swore
that if this was done, I would surely see
a ripe old age – loved by my people too
and die in my own palace peacefully."
"May the gods ensure this will all come true"
answered his faithful wife and kissed his head.
As they talked, two servants worked at speed
laying soft rugs on their master's bed.
When this was finished, one went down to lead
her lord and lady by soft candlelight
to their chamber, to rest there for the night.

So, they lay together on their bed
mingling once more in love's abandoned play
and afterwards lay sated, head to head.
Downstairs, Telemachus moved all away
from the dining hall; harper, and maids too,
so, no noise would disturb the pair upstairs.
Then with his time for rest long overdue,
he and his two friends dragged benches and chairs
as makeshift beds and slept there in the hall.
Meanwhile lord and lady turned round once more,
and afterwards, in mutual recall
told their stories: her days made hard and sore
by suitors, each one without fear or grace,
each one pressing to take her husband's place.

Taking his time, Odysseus told his wife
his adventures since leaving Troy behind
from the Cicones [start of all his strife]
the Lotus eaters, drugged in will and mind,
the dreadful one-eyed Cyclops in his cave.
On Aeolus Isle, at last sweet sanctuary
and homeward bound when gale and mountain wave
drove his comrades backwards across the sea.
Next the Laestrygorians, so pitiless
so many gallant comrades butchered there.
Next to Circe's land, the lovely goddess
turned his men into pigs and laid a snare
for Odysseus too, but all turned out well
for his crew when Circe removed her spell.

He told her of his time among the shades,
meeting Tiresias, the soothsayer,
then conversing with his long dead comrades,
and his mother too [he'd been unaware
that years before she had joined the dead].
He told her of the Sirens' melody
of Charybdis and Scylla; of how he led
his remaining crewmen across the sea;
of how his shipmate, against his own advice,
out of greed killed the cattle of the gods,
and how each one paid the final price,
capsized by Zeus; how he, against all odds
grabbed on to wreckage; came safely through
the one survivor of his gallant crew.

After days at sea, at last he came ashore
where Calypso kept him trapped for seven years.
Although she wanted him and pressed him sore
to be her husband, he ignored her tears,
her promises and all her magic arts.
At last, the gods forced her to let him free
and he reached the Phaeacians whose generous hearts
made him welcome, then set him to sea
with gifts of precious clothes and bronze and gold
and safe passage to his native land.
Satisfied that his story had been told
he drowsed mid word, holding his sweet wife's hand.
She smiled, watching her husband sink to deep
and dreamless rest, into a well earned sleep.

Athena, who was watching from above,
waited until she thought the time was right
[when Odysseus had his fill of sleep and love]
and opened his eyes to dawn's rosy light.
"You and I have endured much suffering,"
he said "let's look to better times ahead.
In time, I'll sail away on raids to bring
back animals to field or fold or shed
that the suitors have taken in their greed.
The locals too must also pay their share.
But first things first I must now speed
to see my father, worn by age and care.
I will head up country so he can see
his son is home and end his misery."

"You've proved in many ways that you are wise
but I warn you; ensure you stay inside
your room today. As soon as it's sunrise,
word will travel how all the suitors died.
Except for your maids, speak to no one here."
With that he left her, descending to the hall
to wake the swineherd and Telemachus there.
Spurred into action by Odysseus' call
they armed themselves and marched out hurriedly,
just as the sun rose in the eastern sky
with Odysseus leading the team of three.
In case they should be seen by mortal eye
Athena fashioned darkness to drop down
around them all, 'till they had left the town.

Finale

Meanwhile the suitors' ghosts were called away
by Hermes who led them with his golden wand.
They moved about him as he made his way
squeaking as bats do, flitting around
a cavern's underworld with faint high cries.
He led the suitors on and so they sped
past sombre shores and ever darkening skies
until they reached the kingdom of the dead.
A gathering of shades assembled there,
Achilles, Patrocles were side by side
with Antilochus and Ajax stood near
as well as Agamemnon who had died
not in battle glory on land or sea
but in his home, through his wife's treachery.

Agamemnon turned and spoke enviously
to Achilles and Ajax at his side
"You both were lost in battle; as for me
my death will be remembered without pride,
slaughtered in cold blood." He held his head
in deep shame when he spoke. Hermes came by
with restless suitors flitting overhead.
The three great heroes raised a greeting cry
and Agamemnon, seeing one he knew
called out "Amphímedon! What brings you down
to these dark halls of death with this young crew?
A battle? A siege of some fortressed town?
Shipwrecked on open sea with no land near?
Let me know, what reason brings you here?"

"You are my brother's son and should recall
your father. Menelaus, travelled with me
to Ithaca. There in Odysseus' hall
we urged him [succeeding eventually]
to fight with us at Troy." The new shade said
"Agamemnon, you tell the truth I know.
As to what brings us here among the dead
I'll tell you clearly and I'll tell you now.
After Odysseus had been gone for years
we assembled to court Penelope.
She put us off with shows of smiles and tears
not saying yes or no. But we could see
that this lady was trying every way
to dash our hopes by tricks or by delay."

"One of her many tricks I now can tell.
She placed her loom before us in the hall
with large baskets of fabric there as well.
"Young men," She cried, "let me inform you all.
Now that my lord is dead, I'll choose a mate
out of the suitors here who seek my hand.
But before I marry, you must all wait
until this weaving's done for I have planned
to weave a funeral shroud. You may well know
Odysseus' father Laertes has been ill.
My good name in this place would be dragged low
if he lay unshrouded. That is my will."
She touched our hearts then with her sighs and tears,
We little knew she'd fool us for three years."

"And so, she did her weaving every day
but undid her hard work by torch light,
fooling us for three years in this way.
Then one of her maids came to us one night
with the secret. We rushed up to her room
to find her unravelling what she had done
throughout that day and evening from her loom.
She had to finish it. When it was spun
we thought our waiting surely had to end.
Out of the blue, Odysseus now came back
arriving at this court, led by a friend.
He was well disguised, leaning on a stick,
dressed in beggar's rags and smelly too.
He perched there in the hall among our crew."

"We jeered at him, took potshots at him too.
Patient as a stone, he bore it all.
With Telemachus and another two
he planned to kill us in the dining hall.
First his son hid all our weaponry,
then his wife set up a test next day,
involving strength and skill at archery,
using Odysseus' bow. There was no way
we could even string the mighty bow.
The tramp took it up despite our mutterings.
He strung it easily and then aimed low
to send the arrow clearly through the rings,
then laid out arrows on a windowsill
while we were wondering at this show of skill."

"He sent another arrow on its way
through the throat of Antinoos. Then he cried
I am Odysseus! All of you will pay
for what you've done. Even though we tried
to hide ourselves, arrows sped through the air
from his bow, killing us one by one.
His son, swineherd and cowherd helped him there
and some god too; for when all was done
the hall ran red, with corpses piled up high.
So now you know how our deaths took place.
Unattended, our bloodstained bodies lie
outside that hall, without a farewell embrace
from friend or family. It is not right
to deny these dead young men their due rite."

But Agamemnon smiled and then exclaimed
"Ah Odysseus, Laerte's son, my friend!
What a wife you chose! Her name will be proclaimed
by the gods above and heard from end
to end of this wide world, on land and sea
as the model of a faithful wife.
unlike my wife, steeped in adultery,
who coldly killed her husband with a knife."
Meanwhile Odysseus and the other three
reached Laerte's home and Odysseus cried
"Prepare a meal inside the house. I'll see
my father first. He spends his time outside
I'm told, removing weed and briar and stone
from the orchard here, working all alone."

Odysseus found his father spading soil
around the base of a young fruit tree.
The old man stood, intent upon his toil,
his clothing patched, bound tight below the knee
to protect against briars and nettle sting.
He wore a cap of mourning on his head
and looked ground down by grief and suffering.
His son paused by a pear tree. There he shed
a tear to see his father, worn and weak.
Should he tell him first that he was his son
or draw him slowly out and let him speak?
Thinking quickly, he chose the second one
and walked ahead. Laertes worked away
with spade in hand, banking up the clay.

Approaching his father, Odysseus said
"You are a skilful gardener, I see.
Every plant and shrub, every flower bed
is well looked after, but it seems to me,
and please don't take offence at what I say
that you don't look after yourself at all.
Your clothes are badly torn, grubby and gray.
What lord would let an aged servant fall
into such neglect – if a slave you are?
By your bearing, one might well suggest
you're used to better living and richer fare
than a lowly servant might expect.
But if you're a slave, then if that's the case,
tell me who is the master of this place?"

"And tell me this as well. I need to know.
Is this Ithaca? Earlier today
I met a man who told me this was so,
but as we stood and talked, to my dismay
he turned aside with anger on his face
when I asked about another native here.
That man I welcomed to my own palace,
a son of Laertes. He and I grew near
during the time that he remained with me.
When he left, I gave him gifts; bars of gold;
a sliver winebowl with fine filigree
rings and robes and a silver chest to hold
these treasures. I gave four well trained servants too
before he sailed away with his own crew."

His father's eyes filled up with bitter tears.
"You're in the proper place, but take great care
for he has not been home for several years
and dangerous men have taken over here.
If he were here today, he'd surely see
that you were given gifts to match your own
fine presents and your hospitality.
But tell me this; how many years have flown
since you met that visitor? He was my son
destined to die far from his native land
after long travel, but now his race is done.
My wife and I have had no chance to stand
with his own wife, no chance to kiss his head
and close his eyes. So much is due the dead."

"Who are you – of what land and family?
Where have you moored the ship that brought you here?
Where is your crew, or did you come by sea
on someone else's ship?" "You will hear
my story" quick witted Odysseus cried
"My name is Eperitus, a king's son
from Alybas. Buffeted by wind and tide,
I was swept off course. When the gale was done,
we berthed near to here in a quiet bay.
As for your son, five long years have passed
since he left our court. Bound for death you say?
Yet landbirds flew right across his mast
as he sailed away; a lucky sign it's said
of safe sailing and happy days ahead."

Laertes bent and groaning heavily
scooped up grey dust and spilled it on his head.
His son, knowing he could not stand and see
his father so distraught, kissed him and said
"My dear father. I have come back to you.
I've killed the suitors, so no grieving now."
Laertes answered him. "If this is true
give me some proof of it so I can know
my son is here." Odysseus made reply
"I will give two signs as proof of what I say.
First of all; this boar's mark on my thigh.
I suffered on a summer's hunting day
on Mount Parnassus – you had sent me there
to my grandfather. Look – the scar is here."

"The second proof grows all around us here.
When I was a small boy, you promised me
ten apple trees, forty fig, thirteen pear
and fifty rows of vine. Each vine and tree
you planted was a present for your boy."
The old man slumped; Odysseus held him tight
until he stood again, weeping tears of joy.
Suddenly his eyes widened in fright.
"You have told me the suitors are all dead
and by your hand. We will pay the cost
if their families gather here to shed
our blood in vengeance for sons that they have lost."
Odysseus hugged his father and replied
"Be not afraid; the gods are on our side."

The pair returned to where the other three
were roasting pork, preparing wine and bread.
Laertes bathed, and anxious to be free
of his rags and the mourning cap on his head,
dressed in new clothes. Athena, standing near,
filled out his withered frame, his arms and thighs.
Seeing him transformed, Odysseus cried "It's clear
some god has changed you right before my eyes!"
"I wish I was young again" his father cried.
"I could have helped you, father beside son
when you killed the suitors, stood by your side."
With all the mealtime preparations done
the five sat down on bench or stool or seat
enjoying the wine and the crisp hot meat.

As they feasted old Dolios appeared,
work stained from the field, his sons by his side.
He was Laertes' right-hand man. He stared
at Odysseus, then kissed his head and cried
"You have come home again! Can this be true?
We had lost hope, thinking you were dead.
Does Queen Penelope know this news too
or should we send a messenger ahead?"
Odysseus said "She knows that I am here
so there's no need to send out anyone.
But tell your sons to pull the benches near
for there's another battle to be won
should the suitors' families track us down,
knowing that we have come here from the town."

Meanwhile the news spread through the countryside
of what had happened on the previous night
and how the suitors and the twelve maids died
at Odysseus' hands. By morning light
a murmuring crowd gathered before the hall.
Seeing the bloody corpses piled up high
where they had been thrown, at the courtyard wall
each one stood stunned, then each one's heaving cry
joined a bitter chorus of rage and loss.
They carried off the bodies, one by one
some to be buried nearby, some brought across
by ferry to their homelands. When this was done
they took their places in grim assembly;
each one numbed in silent misery.

Old Eupeithes rose to address then all.
Antinoos was his son, the first man slain
by Odysseus in the dining hall.
"My friends" he said "We have been wronged again
by that bastard! Years ago he sailed to Troy
taking young men from this place. All were lost.
Now he's returned, he's killed my only boy
and your sons too! He must pay the cost.
Let's move without delay or he'll take flight
or live in shame, mocked by everyone.
Vengeance is our duty, and our right.
As for me, I'd prefer to join my son
in the underworld than to stand aside
and do nothing. It's time to act", he cried.

His heartfelt words moved each and every one
but two others addressed the crowd as well.
First Medon spoke. "While killings were being done
in the hall, I saw, as each young man fell,
a god, disguised as Mentor, standing there:
opposing a god is not within man's right."
Now Halithérses cried "My friends, beware
of reckless action now. Night after night,
your dog rough sons lived lives of gluttony
and dishonoured a wise and faithful queen.
Listen well and heed my prophecy
as a future vision that I have seen.
Let vengeance rest, or you will join the dead
before this day is done," Halithérses said.

Though some of them agreed with what was said,
the rest grabbed their helmets, shields, swords and spears
to act on Eupeithes' words instead.
In high Olympus, Athena voiced her fears
to mighty Zeus. "Father, be my guide.
Should we end this strife; otherwise, we face
more killings and reprisals. Enough have died,
enough blood has been shed in this place."
"My child" he said, "the only proper way
is to let Odysseus remain as king.
Meanwhile I will act to clear away
all memory of each death and so bring
peace between the warring factors there:
Daughter, go and make all sides aware!"

She left Olympus, flashing through the sky
to stand, quite unseen, at Odysseus' side.
They had finished eating when a hue and cry
disturbed their ease. The group now rushed outside
and saw the townsmen marching up the lane.
Arming themselves, they went to meet the foe
joined by Athena, now disguised again
as Mentor. "Telemachus, you must show
true courage here," Odysseus urged his boy.
"Father I won't disgrace our family,"
Telemachus said. Laertes cried with joy
"What a proud day it is for me to see
my son and grandson standing head-to-head
to prove their valour now," the old man said.

Athena whispered in Laertes' ear
"Take your trusted lance and aim it straight."
Suddenly empowered, the old man threw his spear
at Eupeithes, standing at the gate.
It struck him on the face, right through his cheek
on one side and punched through the other one.
His mouth opened slowly as if to speak
then he dropped dead, falling like a stone.
Odysseus and his friends charged straight ahead
intent on killing each man in their way,
but Athena roared, striking such utter dread
that both sides stood. "Now throw your arms away
and go back to the town." the goddess cried.
"End this fighting! Too many men have died."

They did as they were told, white faced with dread
dropping swords and spears and shields to the ground.
Now rearing like an eagle overhead
Odysseus poised again to strike them down.
Just then a thunderbolt flamed through the sky,
sent by Zeus and sizzled at Athena's side.
She stopped Odysseus in his tracks with a cry.
"Odysseus my friend. I have been your guide
since you sailed to Troy twenty years ago.
Call off this battle now or you will see
my father's rage." Odysseus bowed down low
and yielded to divine authority.
Both parties swore to terms of peace; to mend
past disputes; bringing this feud to an en

Glossary

Achilles
When Achilles was born his mother, Thetis, attempted to make her baby boy immortal by dipping him in the black waters of the River Styx, while holding him by the heel. This one part of his body left untouched by the water became Achilles' only weak point- his Achilles heel. Years later he becomes the Greek hero at the ten-year Trojan War. He is eventually killed there by an arrow which strikes him in the heel.

Aeolus
Keeper of the winds and ruler of the floating island of Aeolia. He could choose to create storms at will.

Agamemnon
King of Mycenae and commander in chief of the Greek army during the Trojan War. On his return from the war, he was murdered by his wife, Clytemnestra, and her lover Aegisthus.

Ajax
Prince of Salamis who fought at Troy. He carried the body of his friend, Achilles, from the battlefield. He killed himself when the armour of Achilles was given to Odysseus rather than to him following a vote called among the Greek leaders to settle the issue.

Alcinous

King of Schleria and ruler of the Phaeacians, a tribe
famous for their hospitality to sea travellers.
He offers shelter and generous gifts to Odysseus before his
return to Ithaca.

Antinous

The most arrogant and cruel of the suitors. He is the first
to be killed by Odysseus.

Apollo

God of prophecy, healing, music, and archery.
He supported the Trojans in the war against the Greeks.

Arête

Queen of the Phaeacians. Renowned for her wisdom.
She receives Odysseus as an honoured guest in her court.

Athena

Goddess of wisdom and war. She was the favourite child
of Zeus, leader of all the gods.
As protectress of Athens she supported the Greeks during
the Trojan War.
Athena helps Odysseus and his son Telemachus from the
start to the end of the Odyssey.

Calypso

When Odysseus is shipwrecked on the island of Ogygia,
home of the nymph Calypso, she falls in love with him.
She offers him an escape from ageing and death if he stays
with her. After seven years she is commanded by Zeus to

let Odysseus sail home to his wife *Penelope.*
It is said that Calypso later kills herself, unable to bear being parted from Odysseus.

Circe

A minor goddess and enchantress, living alone on the island of Aeaea. Here she turns travellers who land on her shores into pigs, lions and wolves.
Protected against her magic by the herb, moly, Odysseus lives with Circe for a year.

Charon

For a fare of one silver coin placed in the mouth of a corpse, Charon would ferry the dead person in his boat across the River Styx, which separate the world of the living from the world of the dead.

Charybdis

A sea monster in the shape of a dangerous whirlpool guarding the narrow entrance of the Messina Straits. Passing ships are pulled down into this whirlpool.

Demodocus

The blind musician at the court of King Alcinous and Queen Arête, who delights Odysseus with his songs about the Trojan War.
It is believed that Demodocus represents Homer himself.

Eumaeus

The loyal swine herd of Odysseus who helps him overthrow the suitors.

Eurycleia
Odysseus's childhood nurse. When Odysseus returns
home in disguise, she recognises him by a scar on his
thigh.

Eurylochus
Second in command in Odysseus' crew. He challenges the
leadership of Odysseus and stirs up trouble.

Eurymachus
A young nobleman from Ithaca and one of the suitors.
He is deceitful and manipulative. Penelope's maid
Melantho is his lover.

Hades
God of the dead and ruler of the underworld where he
rules with Persephone. Like Death itself he is stern and
pitiless, unmoved by prayer or sacrifice.

Helen
Queen of Sparta and wife of Menelaus. She was said to
have been the most beautiful woman in the world.
Her abduction by Prince Paris led to the Trojan War.
After the fall of Troy rejoined Menelaus in Sparta.

Helios
God of the sun. His sun chariot, driven by four winged
horses, drove across the sky each day, starting each
morning in the east and arriving at evening time in the
west.
His herds of 350 sheep and 350 roamed the land of Sicily.

Heracles

Son of Zeus, with superhuman strength, he was the greatest of the Greek heroes. He wore a lion skin and carried a huge club as a weapon.

Hermes

God of travel, trade, and fertility. He was the patron of travellers He was also the messenger of the gods, bringing information or warnings from Mount Olympus to those living on earth.

Laertes

King of Ithaca. Broken-hearted over the twenty-year absence of his only son, Odysseus, he is left alone when his wife Anticleia dies from grief. Leaving his palace, he keeps to himself working as a gardener. When Odysseus returns, he helps his son confront the families of the dead suitors who seek revenge for their sons' deaths.

Medon

Odysseus' herald. He was forced to serve the suitors. When Odysseus returns to Ithaca, he spares the life of Medon.

Melanthius

The chief goatherd of Ithaca. He betrays Odysseus and sides with the suitors but is hacked to death for his betrayal.

Melantho

A servant in the court of Penelope. She is the mistress of Eurymachus, one of the suitors. She is hanged with the other eleven maids who consorted with the suitors.

Menelaus

King of Sparta. He married Helen who was taken by Prince Paris to Troy. This was the cause of the ten-year Trojan War. Helen returned with Menelaus when Troy fell.

Mentor

When Odysseus leaves Ithaca to fight in the Trojan War, he places Mentor, a trusted servant, in charge of training his only son, Telemachus, so that the youngster can learn the skills he will need to rule Ithaca in his father's absence. We now use the word mentoring to describe someone who shares wisdom and experience with a less experienced person.

Naussica

Daughter of King Alcinous and Queen Arête. She befriends Odysseus when he is shipwrecked on Schleria.

Nestor

King of Pylos. An expert charioteer, he fought in the Trojan War and returned safely home.
He was noted for his wisdom and justice.

Odysseus
Leaving his wife Penelope and their new-born son, Telemachus, he sets sail from Ithaca, leading a fleet of twelve ships to fight in the Trojan War. A brave and cunning strategist, his trick involving a wooden horse enables the Greek army to capture Troy.
His ten-year return from Troy is called The Odyssey... a name we use to this day to describe a long, challenging journey.

Patrocles
Close friend of Achilles, accompanying him during the Trojan War. He was killed by Hector towards the end of the siege of Troy and was buried beside Achilles.

Peisistratus
Youngest son of King Nestor of Pylos. He becomes a friend of Telemachus and travels with him seeking news of Odysseus.

Penelope
Wife of Odysseus and mother of Telemachus.
Her patience and cunning help her out manoeuvre the suitors while Odysseus is away. The challenge she sets these young men [the test of the bow] is key to their eventual overthrow. The other challenge she sets Odysseus, [the test of the bed] It proves to her that her long absent husband has returned home.

Persephone
Goddess of the underworld, having been captured by
Hades and forced to become his wife. She is the
patron of vegetation and the changing seasons.

Philoetius
The faithful cowherd of Odysseus. He remained loyal to
his master during Odysseus' twenty-year absence from
Ithaca. Along with Eumaeus he helps Odysseus to
overthrow the suitors.

Polyphemus
A Cyclops from Sicily, Polyphemus was the one-eyed son
of Poseidon, god of the sea. He traps Odysseus and his
men in his cave, eating six of them. In revenge Odysseus
and his crew leave Polyphemus blinded and make their escape.

Poseidon
God of the sea. and brother of Zeus. He tries to destroy
Odysseus on several occasions in revenge for the blinding
of his son Polyphemus. His symbol was the trident which
he used to stir up storms at sea and earthquakes.

Scylla
A sea monster with twelve feet and six heads. Each head
carried three rows of razor-sharp teeth. From her cave on
the Straits of Messina, she devoured passing sailors
including six of Odysseus' crew.

Sirens

A sea creature with the body of a bird and the head of a woman, who brought sailors to their deaths with their bewitching song. In the Odyssey, two Sirens attempt to lure Odysseus and his crew.

Teirisias

The prophet of the god Apollo. He was struck blind as a young man for watching the goddess Athena as she bathed. Teirisias is a complex figure in Greek mythology, positioned somewhere between gods and mortals, between male and female, between this world and the world of the dead. Although blind he has inner vision which helps him see into the future. Odysseus must travel to the Underworld to seek Teirisias' advice on how he may get home to Ithaca.

Telemachus

Son of Penelope and Odysseus. His father leave home when Telemachus is an infant. When he comes of age, Telemachus travels for news of his missing father. After their reunion he helps Odysseus overcome the suitors who are unwelcome guests at the court of Ithaca.

Zeus

Father of the gods on Mount Olympus and ruler of all humans. His symbols included an eagle and a thunderbolt. He had the power of sending thunder and lightning storms.